COMING OUT OF WITCHCRAFT

COMING OUT OF WITCHCRAFT

Faith Aponte

Introduction

Introduction

Coming out of witchcraft and giving my life to Jesus wasn't the first option I had in mind, I had to go through a lot of hoops, and what I thought I knew I didn't know. My prayer is that this book reaches and touches the lost, broken, used, abused, and unwanted. Allow me to say you aren't alone as well as you have a purpose. Hi, my name is Faith. I was into witchcraft for years as an eclectic witch. I was sexually assaulted at the age of 16 and asked why would Jesus let this happen to me. I got into witchcraft making sure I manifested safety, wealth, and whatever my heart desires to make sure that it will never happen again. Later I found out that playing with tarot cards, spirit boxes, zodiacs, crystals, and way more left me more depressed, stressed, and demonically oppressed. The Lord has placed on my heart to expose the devil and witchcraft for what it is. If you are ready and tired of manifesting and taking over, come all you weary for the lord may give you rest! I pray this book guides you into peace and your spiritual eyes will be open in Jesus' name!

Contents

My Testimony

My Testimony

I was the black sheep of my family, considering how I was adopted into a Caucasian family from birth and me being an African-American, it had its differences. My adoptive parents did a great job raising me so well that I didn't see color. My adopted parents are my parents to me and my brothers and sister are my siblings to me. My Dad had a Family Business called Burrington associated passed down from my grandfather, but unfortunately around 2015, the business shut down so which meant we had to downsize. That was hard because I had to leave all of my friends. I had to change my school, I normally went to a predominantly white school, but I went to a completely different school with a variety of different races and kids in the school district.

My parents stopped going to church, but I didn't think anything of it I just thought it was because they got tired of waking up early as much as I did so I didn't complain. I was a social butterfly. I did a lot of school activities and I was well involved. I was a part of the color guard track and cheerleading. I kept myself very busy throughout the school year. At the end of middle school eighth grade, I was sexually assaulted by a classmate. I'm going to name this classmate John Doe for the sake of confidentiality. I was quick to make friends, considering I was the only one left in my house out of all my siblings because everyone else moved out and was grown and started there own lives away from home that left me with no one to talk to. This girl who I wanted to hang out with one day, who lived behind me at the time, lets say her name is Becky for the sake of confidentiality. Becky Invited me to go to the movies with her I didn't even know Becky I only knew her because of school, and she lived the street down behind me I was desperate for friends so I decided to go. My dad dropped me off at the movies and to my surprise Becky and her boyfriend was there and John Doe was there I didn't think anything of it. We got our tickets and we went to go see fast and furious seven during the whole time at the movies I just felt uncomfortable, because John Doe kept trying to touch me kiss me and his breath reeks of onions like he just got done eating a hoagie. When the movie was over my dad picked us up and dropped us off back home we all decided to hang out and play tag. I ran into my best friends house that lived down the street I asked her if she wanted to play and she said no. I asked if any of her siblings wanted to play, and a few of them decided to play with us. It was my turn for my team to hide, so I asked Becky if I could put my phone on her porch because my pants pocket wasn't deep enough to hold my phone and my phone kept weighing down my pants as a ran. I left my phone and the movie theater bucket on Becky's porch. We was having fun on that spring afternoon but it was starting to get dark. My best friend's siblings had went inside and I went to go grab my phone off beck's porch but John doe ran in front of me grabbed my phone and started to run and said "if you want it come and get it." So I continued to run after him he lead me to the park with him sitting on the swings. " look its getting dark I want my phone back." I told him. He continued to ignore me and then proceeded to ask me questions " Tell me about yourself?" He asked. "Well, I'm adopted and I moved here from Pottsgrove to Pottstown. I answered." " what's it like being adopted?" "it's okay I guess.. Can I please have my phone back?" John doe then replied " If you want to jump up and get it. Me being short and him being tall there's no way I would be able to reach my phone. I tried jumping up. Then John doe grabbed me stick his hands down my pants and started to stick his fingers up my vagina. I began to struggle and tried to stick my hand in my pants to push his fingers out of me. I tried to get away but there was no point he was faster then me and I was scared he wasn't going to give me my phone back unless he had sex with me. He asked me where I wanted to have have sex I told him "you can't put your dick in my vagina because my mom checks me." So he ended up putting it in my anus. I told I'm I didn't want to do this and that it hurts and I started to cry with tears coming down my eyes. "I'm almost there." John doe replied. When he was done he asked me if I liked it. I lied and I said yes and he gave me my phone back and I walked one way as he walked the other way. Tears ran from my face as I walked home every step I made I was in pain. that event had me so lost, broken, depressed, and alone, I kept my sexual assault from my parents for three days, I planned to keep it a secret forever, but the only person I told was my best friend at the time. My friend notice how different I was acting in school, and eventually told my mom shortly after. When my best friend told my mom, I hated her, I was beyond upset with her to the point where I couldn't even explain the rage I had at that time when she told my mother, my mom was scheduled to babysit my niece at the time so my mom immediately called my sister-in-law to pick up my niece then called the police. bursting through the door and yelling "What happened?!" my sister-in-law's eyes filled with tears and a broken concerned voice and all I could say back with a broken voice and tears coming down, my eyes were " I got hurt."

Then the police showed up and I gave a statement as much as I could. The police told my parents to take me to the hospital to get a rape kit done and they immediately rushed me over to the Children's Hospital in Philly where I saw so many doctors and was given shots, pills, and had to answer so many questions. Through that chapter in my life, I spoke with so many people, doctors, lawyers, therapists, counselors, and detectives my life was a mess and was completely turned upside down. After going through all that I just went back to school and pretended as if nothing happened but unfortunately, because my persecutor was a student and it was a small town and he wasn't taken into custody yet word got out that it was consensual. I had students come up to me, mostly boys, saying "Oh faith I didn't know you got down like that, you freaky." as they looked at me up and down. I was in cheerleading so even some of the people in the squad spoke about me behind my back. I just tried to keep it together the best I could and keep myself busy and away from home.

The 8th grade formal rolled around and because the majority of the popular kids were just picking on me I decided to go to formal with a boy named Jovaun. I asked him to Formal because he just seemed safe and pure he wasn't interested in clicks and being well-known so I went to the dance together and we started dating shortly after. I was falling in love I told him everything and went to his house almost every day. When we hung out we didn't do anything he just played his video games most of the time and I watched but he was so simple and just peaceful and a great listener. I worked at Papa John's at the time and I was doing horrible at my job because of the trauma I was going through just couldn't focus I felt as if I was missing something so I ended up having sex at a very young age of 16, thinking being with Jovaun would be able to fill a void in my life that I was missing hoping I could replace what was taken from me.

Speaking with the detectives and lawyers my story wasn't enough for them to win the chase because in the end, it looked like it was consensual and that I allowed him to have sex with me willingly So John Doe was able to still go to school and walk around town. My principal at the time was well aware of the situation and John doe wasn't at the school anymore but he came up to visit friends time to time. one day him and a group of friends followed me and I quickly look at the principle and told him " he is behind me." and I kept walking I didn't want to walk home because he knew where I lived so I walked to Jovaun's house.

That same day after school I went to his house and his mom was under the influence of something because of me being pretty much sheltered from this. I wasn't sure what was going on. She got very angry and started cursing at Jovaun about one thing or another. Jovaun began to cry so I hugged him and told him "It's okay. " He hugged me back. "Don't comfort him! " his mom yelled. So I replied and said "Why aren't you doing it? "Let's just say she didn't like that comment very much. Her anger grew and she yelled at me to get out of her house. I was about to leave out the door but she yelled " I heard you weren't even raped! " I blacked out and started to punch her next thing you know me and my boyfriend's mom was in a first fight. Jovaun quickly came outside and pulled us apart. With both of us both being small it was easy for Jovaun to pick us up. Later that night after that I got a text message from Jovaun saying that we couldn't date anyone. I felt as if I lost everything, my peace, my comfort I was broken and I honestly didn't even want to live anymore.

Shortly after that, I tried to kill myself and I ended up hospitalized for a week and three days I stayed at Horsham clinic. My experience there was horrible. I got in there at 3am very tired and they woke me up at 8am my first day I was extremely exhausted. I met lots of people all with different stories but I never cared to ask what there story was. There was girls in my pod that was angry and some just depressed. I feel as if i just had to fake a smile the whole time just so I could get out of there. One day during my stay my mom came to visit me. "You got to get me out of here", I said to my mom." "I can't sign you out of here my mom said to me." Her and I were conversing about one thing or another and she said "You're manipulative." All I could remember at the moment is that I passed out and I could hear my mom softly calling my voice faith....faith are you okay? I woke up frantically and told her I just passed out. I was so upset at that point that I wasn't dreaming and I was really stuck in the mental hospital I took the plastic chair and threw it across the room not caring about the other patients and there parents I ended up crying and screaming Get Me OUT OF HERE! I punched the tv plastic plexiglass lining and all the screws came out of it and a couple of the patients took the screws and ran to there room to self harm. It was a long 10 days on my last day I finally got to talk to the main therapists that determined if I could leave or not and I remember her saying to me " your not crazy faith me reading your chart is like me reading a book" that statement bothered me " I'm glad my life is an amusement for you me thinking in my head but still smiling because my goal is to get out of this place. I got out I went back to school and I met this girl and I fell in love with her I told her everything and everything we eventually started dating. I trusted no man at this point. My girlfriend always knew how to keep it fun and chill and we always were laughing and acting stupid. When I was 18 I thought I was grown and I moved into a crappy one-bedroom infested with bedbugs and moved there with my girlfriend and her brothers. In my downtime, I was studying new age dark magic, light magic, anything.

I wanted to make sure that no one would be able to kill my joy or my relationship. I ended up worshiping false Gods that I believed were lined up with my zodiac sign, I charged crystals under the sun and the moon. collected rainwater and did new moon bath rituals, new age magic and more I was always punctual with casting spells in there appropriated time window to make sure for the best so called results.

Unknown seed planted

Well, Papa Johns didn't work out so I ended up getting a job at McDonald's my Girlfriend and I both worked there. We were there so often we began to build relationships with the regular customers. There was this one customer in particular that caught my eye and she would just sit there swatting the air as if there were flies around her and she did it all the time . I didn't think anything of it because hey I did work at McDonalds and all this lady would do is sit and read the bible. Day after day the homeless lady would come in and do the same thing. I went up to her and gave her food and she told me that she can't eat any meat. I asked the lady "Well then what would you like to eat then? " all she asked for was some apple slices so I gave her just that.

The next day the Lady was at McDonald's again swatting flies and reading her bible. It was the middle of my shift and we had extra food so I gave her food. " I can't eat," she replied" So I burst out and asked, "

How can you be picky and homeless? I'm just trying to help." The lady explained to me that it's part of her religion. " ooh I see you Muslim or something?" " She said "No Christian." shift after shift day after day I would see this lady more and more and then the season grew cold so one day I asked my girlfriend hey do you think this lady can stay with us because it's cold she agreed so I went over to the lady and invited her over. She slept on the floor. It was a very tight squeeze but we made it work.

I realized that there weren't any flies in my house so I asked her "Why do you do this?" As I swatted over my head she explained to me that her brother was a very evil person and practices witchcraft and voodoo and put a spell on her and that it feels like bees are around her all the time and the only time she catches a break is when she reads the holy bible. " Well, you came to the right place, hold on." I smiled and ran to my room and grabbed all of my new-age stuff. " I'm a good witch, all you need is some sage and you will be good," I explained. The lady seemed desperate to try anything but also reluctant that it was witchcraft. She followed me into the bathroom and she sat on the edge of the bathtub. I began to burn the sage and make circles around her as I chanted Break!, Break! Break every curse! I even handed her crystals and looked up spells then the lady got un-comfy and said it's just making it worse and she started swatting even more. So began to blow out the candles and smudge the sage and apologize to her. Three days passed and the lady went on her way and I never saw her again.

As I got older I grew curious about my biological mother so I got the court information about my mother from my mom. I found out my mother and Father had a history of drugs as well as my grandmother who has an alcohol addiction. I got a hold of my brother on Instagram and spoke with him and my girlfriend and I planned a day to go to Chester Pa to see my family. I had an awesome time meeting everyone. My sister even took us out to eat and we got an Uber to the restaurant but we ran out of money so we had to walk back but I didn't mind we were laughing and had a great time I even read Tarot cards to them. I had a great time meeting everyone for the first time.

When I first met my mom she was very skinny but we were just alike. We sounded the same and looked the same. That trip was very special to me but little did I know that would be the first and the last time I would meet my older biological brother Jamal. I was so devastated hearing of his passing. my Grandma informed me that he had passed away on drugs and jumped out of a moving car and he was in Pottsville Pa. I remember crying "Why didn't he call me? I'm in Pottstown. He could have seen me." My heart was broken.

Around this time it was toward the end of the year and everyone was talking about going to college of course I wanted to go so befriended my best friend again and we were talking about college. I brought it up to my parents that I wanted to go but my mom wasn't very supportive "Why don't you go to a community college instead you don't need all the extra stuff and we can't help you pay for it anyway Dad and I are moving to Texas so we can be with my mother ." she explained to me, after her telling me that I just grew very upset and felt like I was a failure and just not smart enough. I took my SAT and only got a 600 on the test. I was so upset I don't want to stay in Pottstown for the rest of my life. I want to grow.

I began to get depressed on top of that and I later contracted the only person I knew and that was Jovaun I haven't talked to him in a hot min let alone seen him so I text him and said " I was wondering if you can take me to the hospital I'm not okay I'm sorry to bother you." He replied almost immediately and replied, "Where are you in on my way." I was sleeping over at my best friend's house that day so it was perfect for me because my girlfriend wouldn't be able to find out where I was. I met up with him and hugged him and he hugged me back and he listened to me and walked me across town in the middle of the night and across town just to come to get me. I went to the hospital that day but they did not admit me.

After that whole breakdown Jovaun and I started talking more and seeing each other more. I even made up with his mom and we are on great terms. I guess Jovaun was in a funk himself. His mom said "Wow, I never saw that boy clean and smile until you came around." The truth came out and my girlfriend went through my phone. I had to pick between Jovaun and my girlfriend and I honestly chose Jovaun. Being with my girlfriend it was a little abusive behind closed doors but we still smiled when we were in public and with Jovaun it was like we would do anything for one another. So I left the apartment and moved to Jovaun at his house.

A lot of my LGBTQ friends I hung out with really did not mess with me after me breaking up with her. I moved all my stuff to Jovaun's house and started to share my hobby of new-age practices with his mom. She was known to be a hippie so she had a lot of interesting books. One of them that caught my eye had a personality test in the book and based on what you got on the test it gave you an identity it gave the option of Star seed, indigo, crystal children, and rainbow children. "Wow I'm a Star seed and I don't come from this world I'm made from stardust and this is why everyone treats me differently?" I thought my 3rd eye was opened and I had my spiritual awakening. I started going to this new-age shop in town that was open at the time on the high street. They had herbs, reiki sessions, tarot readings, tarot cards, crystals, moon water and so much more. We went in one day and I decided to get a reading done.

I wanted to ask about my brother Jamal who had passed away. The medium set the atmosphere and as soon as she said "He is here." I felt a touch on my right shoulder but saw no one. " can you tell him that I love him?" " Is he okay ?" The medium answer " He loves you he said and that he is sorry." "he also is okay he is just thinking about what he has done and thinking over his life." She explained, "How do I know he is near he will send you music she said." Then I started to cry. When Jamal was alive he sent me music all the time through Instagram showing me songs that would cheer him up in hard times. After that, the medium shook the bell and ran out abruptly. "I guess times up then?" I pulled myself together and Jovaun's mom was there waiting for me to get out. She was showing me all the crystals she had picked out. We were ready to check out but the lady that ran the shop was gone. I thought to myself maybe she went to the bathroom. Eventually came out and checked us out but 2 months later the shop closed down and I never saw that lady again.

At this time Jovaun got a job offer from his mother's friend's husband who worked at a manufacturing company this meant that Jovaun was going to move into their house due to the fact that the job was across town and it was easy for him to get a ride and also was a safe place for him to stay through all the chaos at his mom's house. I didn't mind because I was getting ready to start college and attend Kutztown University with my best friend. At that time in my life my belongings were just scattered, some at my boyfriend's house, some at my ex-girlfriend's place, some at my best friend's place and some at my second oldest brother's place. My brother had kidnapped me and taken me into his house because he didn't want me running the streets going house to house in Pottstown so I stayed with them and worked at a little small-town market and worked in the deli until I started college.

The day I started college I was extremely happy to have a place to call my own. The place was an older dorm, in fact, the oldest one on campus, Bonner Hall but it was my space. During my university year, it had its ups and downs. Boy my mom was right, all I did was mess around. I kept myself busy with activities and my best friend ended up growing apart more and more as the college year went on. She had her thing and I had mine. My hobbies included dancing on a hip-hop team called Black Flame partying Thursday through Saturday and of course witchcraft. I met some other people in college. I learned a lot about new age from them and they weren't playing. Eventually, we formed an unspoken covenant: we would go out at midnight and cast spells and read cards and look at the stars and just reflect on the spell and set out intentions.

seed planted with Song

Being a part of the dance team Black Flame we didn't just do hip hop although when I was there God was still planting seeds and I didn't even notice until now. Our dance group was going to perform a praise dance and everyone was required to at least learn it. It wasn't mandatory to perform but it was to learn and we danced to the song

For Your Glory by Tasha Cobbs Leonard. So for a week straight we were learning the dance and that song would get stuck in my head.

Unknown seed planted by protest

One day on a Friday at college there were these protesters holding picket signs saying these rude offensive sayings like " all whores deserve S.T.DS" and " Women belong in the Kitchen. " So much other stuff everyone was yelling and cursing at the Protesters There were Men kissing men, Girls kissing Girls I took out my sage and burned a bundle of it and it burned so fast I have never seen sage burn so fast in my life. I did a ring of sage around the table I was sitting at the near by bench and began to read tarot cards to everyone who wanted a reading done. The protesters' was to talk about Jesus and the word of God and the fact that we are all going to hell. There was one student with a bible and she was kind and was telling the protesters that God loves everyone and that isn't rude like the signs that were held up. I was so caught up with the commotions going on I missed my only chance to visit my boyfriend that weekend because my roommate had left me there. When I got back to my room I started to text everyone that I knew and they all went home for the weekend. I felt stranded. My older brother Collin called me "Hey how is college going ?" Good, I lied. I was failing all my classes except economics passing with a C " Well dude you're going to have to find a way to pay that money back and get a job." He nagged me. "I know.. I know I'm bored because everyone left to go home," I told him. " We'll get a Job." He told me and laughed. I ended that phone call so quick he just made me mad. Lying in my room bored out my mind so I decided to watch porn which gave me the idea to sign up to be a cam model. I would be making money and I wouldn't have to do any real hard work. I waited for my application to get accepted and it took a couple of days and I got accepted. I started to cam and I loved it so many people complimented me and just made me feel good about my body and I made 1000 within the hour. Of course, none of that money went to my student loans, it went to food, alcohol, and the little bookstore town where they sold tarot cards instead.

A CRY FOR HELP

I grew deeper and deeper into a depression I was alone in the door room and my roommate wasn't there I cried and slit my wrist " God why does everyone leave me my parents left me to go to Texas my biological mom left me no one wants me I'm stranded here in the middle of nowhere with no car I hate myself I need your help!" I sent a text message to one of my pagan friends and I didn't realize that she was an anomalous, mandated reporter so next thing I knew the police were in the room and the ambulance was outside of the dorm room and I had to get in the ambulance. I had been through this whole thing before so I knew not to be honest with the doctor. " Do you feel like hurting yourself or causing any harm to others ?" The doctor asked, "No, I'm fine now, " I smiled. The doctor continued to type on his laptop. " Okay, what's your pain tolerance on a scale of 1- 10 ." The doctor asked, " I don't feel anything. I replied to the doctor typing some more. Crap I think I was too honest I thought to myself. An hour went by "Okay we are going to release you and let you go home okay?" The nurse came in with a subtle and sincere voice "Do you want us to call anyone to come pick you up?" She asked "I don't have anyone." I replied with a depressed tone. " okay not to worry we will just call a cab for you okay I hope you feel better." Then the nurse left the room.

I returned to the campus and I didn't leave my room for days then I became very sick. I went to the nurse and she took my temperature and told me not to leave my room and have someone grab my food for me but to stay away from the other students. I told her I didn't have anyone that would do that for me. My roommate is busy and she then explained to me that I don't feel better in 24 hours. I would need to leave the campus. 24 hours passed and I still didn't feel better and I had no money. I tried calling my second oldest brother to see if he could come to pick me up and my sister-in-law said no since she was pregnant and couldn't afford to get sick. I called my parent to send me money and they told me they didn't have it so I called my sugar daddy and he gave me money I got an Uber back to Pottstown and told my boyfriend I was sick his mom set a bed for me in the other room and got me a cold Gatorade I laid there for days.

As I slowly got better and stronger I explained to Jovaun I didn't want to go back to school because I was falling and that I was embarrassed to go back after the ambulance pulled up causing a scene so I applied at McDonald's and never went back to Kutztown again. Jovaun stopped working with his mom's friend's husband because he didn't have his high school diploma so he worked at Papa John's in Norristown. It didn't take long for things to get hectic in the house Jovaun's mom was always arguing with her boyfriend. So Jovaun introduced me to his mom's friend. Finally, her name is Mellissa. This was his other mother to him, a safe place for him to be. She welcomed me to her home and told me that I could stay there if I wanted to if things began to get a little chaotic there. So that's what I did. I met her two daughters Natasha and Alley and of course, I taught them new age and read tarot cards and burned sage.

Melissa told us about a job opportunity in North Carolina to work at a sandwich shop that her friends ran and that they could use some help. The only issue with that is that Jovaun and I don't have a car or a license or a place to stay so that meant we had some work to do. So we started to save as much as we could for the house. Because I was adopted I was truly blessed that my parents saved up money for me to even get a car but they wouldn't release the funds to me until I got my license. My 3rd older brother Jordan drove me around maybe only 2-3 times and Melissa took me out as well because I got my permit. When it came time to take my driving test I was so nervous I kept messing up my left and my right. I didn't stop being the solid line and I failed the test. Now in my defense, I was in Norristown Pa and the solid line wasn't even there and was broken up by a pothole but I digress. Melissa was very supportive and said, "You will get it, you can always try again." I was just down for a whole week I think telling Jovaun the news was harder because it was a lot of pressure on me this is my one ticket out how will I ever be able to do this? "I went upstairs to lie down and just cried " Angels please if you hear me make a way to guide me on where I need to go. " I prayed to them then I fell asleep listening to a meditation, singing bowls to elevate and align my chakras while I fell asleep.

I looked up driving schools near me but the school was very far away so I needed to get a ride. Luckily Melissa was able to take me. I took a class before my test which helped me a lot. The lady showed me what I needed to work on where I was driving for my course. Then I took my test and passed. I was so happy to tell Melissa and Jovaun. 2 weeks later I got a car everything seemed to fall into place.

The angels heard me and helped me so I thought to myself. After all that I ended up going back to Jovaun's mom's house and it was the same stuff differently day arguing back and forth people strung out on God knows what. One day I went up to his mom's room looking for my tarot cards and crystals she sometimes borrows and uses I found my stuff but I also saw a cocaine pipe and lines out on a mirror I grabbed my stuff and told Jovaun what I saw what was up there he called the police to get the drugs removed from the house. Covid was crazy and the town was under curfew So everyone and their mom decided to stay at Jovaun's mother's house. It was just chaotic.

Change in heart

It was a Full moon of a libra and I was reading that it was a perfect time to do spells for balance in my life and breakthrough online so I invited Jovaun's mom to join me but she was too preoccupied and was on a time limit to cast this spell so I just hurried outside. I set out my candles, old pot, herbs, pens, paper, lighter, incense, rocks, and more out on the blanket under the moon and set my sacred space in a sage circle. I looked up at the moon took a deep breath and just cried. " Jesus this shit doesn't work if I am a Libra why is it I need to ask for balance if I am balance?" cried with tears in my eyes." lord I promise you if you just get me out of here I will seek you show me you are real this can't be it for me." Look I will put a stop to it !" I blew out the candles and placed everything in my bag lord please help." I wept and was honest and I just looked at the moon.

Then Jacob made a vow, saying, "If God will be with me and will watch over me on this journey I am taking and will give me food to eat and clothes to wear 21 so that I return safely to my father's household, then the Lord will be my God 22 and this stone that I have set up as a pillar will be God's house, and of all that you give me I will give you a tenth." Genesis 28:20

The Push with Purpose!

It was around 3:00 am that night and Jovaun's mom was asked to log in on her Facebook on my phone. I ignored her question at first then she went upstairs to grab something. " Jovaun I don't want your mom to borrow my phone I don't know what she is going to do with it?" I explained to Jovaun. Jovaun with a blank stare on his face looking at his video game said "Okay." " Faith, can I use your phone?" His mom asked again " Jovaun replied to her "You can't right now she is waiting on a phone call." Jovaun's mom gave a look of disgust and walked away. " Really Jovaun a phone call is like 3:00 in the morning." I hollered at him. Jovaun just stared blankly at his video game. His mom came back angry " I let you leave here for f***ing free and you will not let me use your phone!" She yelled.

I replied With a snarky attitude back.

" You do too. " " What the f**k do you mean I live here for free?!" She yelled back. " Jovaun explained to her that " she lied to section 8 that his younger brother still lives there but doesn't and Jovaun is over the age of 18." After that, it was just a screaming match. " I want you both to leave my house!" Then she started to throw a toolbox at us and other hard objects in our direction but surprisingly it didn't even hit us. Everything fell apart in the air before it could even get to us like there was a wall protecting us. Jovaun and his mother screamed some more that his mom left the house.

God parted the RedSea

The next morning we checked the mail and Jovaun got his sweet stimulus check of $1200 my little $400 dollar paycheck from McDonalds.

So by faith we just set out to North Carolina. I called my oldest brother Colin who lived in Maryland and we decided to stop there for a middle point. I was nervous about driving that far because I was a brand new driver but it was really easy because everyone was on lockdown because of covid so the roads were very clear. The main people on the road were trucks and a few cars. We got to my brother's house safely.

We called our soon-to-be boss and we had a letter of employment with the wages on there for the application process. My brother let us use his desk he had so we could look at apartments in North Carolina. " Wait can we pray first?" I asked, " I don't really do the whole praying thing anymore." Collin replied. "Well God got me this far so I'm going to pray," I said with a stern voice. So we all closed our eyes and bowed our heads. I began to pray " Father God in the name of Jesus please make a way for Jovaun and me so we can start our jobs and stay out of Pottstown Jesus' mighty name I pray amen." "Amen." Everyone said. Within a few moments we came across an apartment complex that was walking distance from one of the shops one of us was going to work at and the first month's rent was free. We quickly filled out an application and called the complex to let them know we filled it out and we got approved within that same hour. That next morning at 5:00am Jovaun and I headed out to North Carolina. We got to the apartment complex and signed the lease in the parking lot and they gave us the keys. We started our new jobs and everything was set.

I would be lying if I stopped my testimony here but I was hard-headed and still read tarot cards, meditated, and just was still all in a new age God kept his promise but I never kept mine. Our jobs got stripped away from us due to poor choices I made, which was not taking Jovaun to work the day after my 21st birthday so we decided to quit because the manager was making Jovaun slice all the meat as a punishment for being late, But God was still faithful we ended up getting raffled into another month rent-free because we paid our rent early which qualified us to get raffled in. Jovaun landed a job at Family Dollar and I was just camming on the side. I applied to a lot of hotels to work there because ever since I was a little girl I wanted to be a hotel manager. I was influenced by shows I would watch as a little girl like Sweet Life of Zack and Cody and Eloise at the Plaza, and anything to do with hotels I just loved. So I applied to everyone in my town and I landed on one the Quality Inn I worked the overnight shift full time and I loved it the only thing that was concerning was that there was no security plus the two sides doors did not lock. But most nights were chill and smooth. Very rarely did I ever have to deal with sketchy people and most people that I did were people strung out on drugs so it wasn't anything new to me.

Watering

One night while working at the hotel I was looking in the bible " lord I don't get this or understand any of this I need you to teach me. "I said. I put down the bible and looked up at my phone. A few minutes passed and a man came in. " Are you checking in or do you have a

reservation?" I asked the man. " reservation," he replied. I got his name information and gave him a key. A few minutes went by and that same man came back down. " My sheets are dirty. Can you go up there and make the bed for me ?" " I'm sorry sir, do you think you can bring down the sheets and I will gladly get you some new ones? I asked him

The man didn't like that I asked him that. " No Here is what you are going to do. You are going to change the sheets and I'm going to follow you and I'm going to watch you do it. He said as he grabbed himself. I immediately felt my heart fall to my stomach and I felt unsafe. I don't want to get hurt again, I thought to myself. " I am not going up there with you. "I told him. "Man Stop being a bitch !" The man angrily yelled at me. At this point, I just wanted to cry but I didn't let a tear come out my eyes. " The man cursed at me picked up the cups of pens and tried to pretend to throw them at me. After that at that point, I was just shaking and I ended up calling the police.

After all the commotion and it was quiet again I locked myself in a vacant room and cried " Lord why does this keep happening? I want this to be free. Why does it seem like everyone sees me as an object? I just need to get baptized so I can be free. New moon bath rituals don't work God I want to learn your word I need a church." I wept.

I pulled myself together and sat back at the front desk. Another man came through the door hours later his name was Chris. "Are you checking in?" I asked him " No I came to tell you about my church" he smiled. Now at this time, I didn't even put two to two together. I just prayed and asked for this because I was still in shock about what had just happened and taken place. " oh okay replied." the man said the service started at 10:30 and we will be happy to have you." he explained with a smile. " I'm sorry I replied I work overnight and I don't want to fall asleep during the sermon I apologize." " No worries, you can always check us out on Facebook." He then proceeded to ask for a pen and paper and wrote down the information and left it with me and left.

I took the paper and I watched an old sermon on their Facebook page. Everything the apostle was saying was everything I needed to hear and just tugged on my spirit at the time.

I ended up quitting that job due to the safety issues went to church and went back to camming online until I got another job and worked back at the sandwich shop. I had never been to an apostolic ministry before where people were speaking in crazy tongues. I found it to be fascinating. I explained to them that I wanted to be baptized and the leaders of the church told me that I needed to take classes first. I attended church and was involved in almost everything Tuesday prayer, Wednesday Bible study, and Sunday service the Lord began to work on my heart I ended up throwing away all my witchcraft items and when I did I was in tears balling my eyes out not because I didn't want to but because I realized it was the reason why I was kept bound in my depression

And I can't do things by myself.

Increase

It was around summer time and I was promoted to management at the sandwich shop I was working at. At the time I had to open the store so I got to the store at 6:00 am just prepping vegetables and baking bread etc. and I didn't get off at work until 4:00 pm. Around this time there was this tent revival the church I was attending was hosting and partnered with another church an hour away in Fayetteville NC and I guess this event was mandatory the Prophet of the house was there for the past 4 days to make sure I went and picked me up straight after work to make sure I went to the event. The tent was outside but it was still set up like a church. It had its stage and musicians, folded chairs set up the same as they would if we were in church inside. The first day the message was great I have seen miracles happen before my eyes there was this lady with a cane and swollen ankles and the apostle laid hands on the Lady and fell they covered her up with a cloth and then the lady got up and began to throw her cane across the tent and began to dance. I was amazed everyone filed up to go get a prophetic word from the Lord. It was my turn. The man of God looked at me and said " The lord wanted me to tell you that the thing that hurt you 6 years ago doesn't have to hurt you anymore and the thing that hurt you 3 months ago doesn't have to hurt you either. Do you understand me? " he asked. " I said yes. " and I sat back down in my chair. I sat down and thought, was it 6 years ago that I was sexually assaulted? I counted and thought, was it 3 months ago with that man at the hotel? I counted again and it was I thought to myself how does he know that? He doesn't have a tarot card, Crystal Ball, or Ouija board and I don't even know him. After the service, I went home then straight to bed then woke up early again for work and like clockwork the Prophet of the house came to pick me up I was exhausted and didn't even When we got there they sang songs and then it was time for the apostle to give the word and everything that man was saying hit my spirit. I even raised my hand in church for the first time Reaching to feel God's touch. It got towards the end and everyone filed up in a line to get their prophetic word but something in me didn't want to go up there. I looked at the Apostle's daughter and she was holding the camera so I decided to hold the camera for her but because deliverance was taking place they told me to turn off the camera for privacy. Everyone has gone up at this point except for me and the apostle looked at me and said into the mic "Some of you aren't going to get your breakthrough and this is your only ticket to it." So I pushed through the feeling of not wanting to go up there and I pushed through the crowd and walked up in front. " Put your hands up," the apostle ordered. I put my hands up about halfway. " No, put your hands up!" The apostle said and pulled my arms over my head. " You were molested when you were a little girl you started dating girls and you were in witchcraft and covenants and you turned so far away from God that the only reason why you went into witchcraft and dated women was that you were trying to protect yourself and you didn't trust God to protect you anymore." "I broke down crying and said it's true" Then all of a sudden I began to feel like I was going to throw up so I ran away from the front of the tent and was gagging. Then the next thing I heard in the mic was " It's a demon so all the staff, the prophets, elders, and prayer warriors got up and walked towards me. As soon as one person touched me I was going in and out of consciousness. I even heard a voice come out of me that wasn't me saying No! Next thing I remember everyone was in a circle shouting Loose her in Jesus' name and everyone was talking at once and I had no control of my body. Things began to calm down and the apostle asked me "What is your name? I said "Faith." He then told me you are free to give God praise. Then the band started to play and I had no idea how to shout. I never had this experience before so I tried my best to shout. Then sat down back at my seat a lot of people in the church came up to me and they shared a little bit of their sexual assault story with me and it helped me to know I wasn't alone. I felt like I was in a Disney movie because everyone started singing "Late in the midnight hour God is going to turn it around, it's going to work in your favor." As they looked at me.

I honestly didn't feel anything after the service except tired and confused as to what just happened. I went to bed that night and woke up the next morning and I took two steps and fell to my knees. "I cried my eyes out " IT'S GONE!!! " " Jesus I was so dark I was so dark I was so dark." I didn't even know how dark I was walking until I was set free.

A Mother that Never lost Faith

THE POWER OF A PRAYING PARENT
God's Promise

A short back story of how we became Faith's parents. Faith was adopted out of the foster system. She has been with us since she was 3 days old and officially became ours when she was 14 months old. God had fulfilled a promise that He made to me sometime earlier as I read Hebrews 11:1. "Now Faith is the substance of things hoped for, the evidence of things not seen." I had been praying for another child. I had 4 biological children and then became sterilized only to regret that decision. So, when I read that scripture, God quickened in my heart that I would get another child. A couple of years later, my husband suggested that we do foster care and we did. To make a long story short, we picked Faith up at the hospital when she was three days old. There was some question at the hospital as to whether her mother had given her a name or not and we were told that we could name her. I knew that her name needed to be a fulfillment of that scripture and so we called her Faith. A week later social workers told us that her mother had indeed given her a name and we would have to use that name. A week after that we were informed that she was being fast-tracked to adoption and asked if we were interested in adopting her. By that point, the whole family was smitten, and we said yes. So, they said that we could call her whatever we wanted but her name would remain her legal name on all documents until she was adopted. I had no idea of the full implications of her name for many years. Even this past year God revealed another impact of her being named Faith. Faith was raised in the church. She had become the "little darling." There were many Sundays that I would hand her off to her big brother and she would be skipped off. Then I would see her in the arms of another church family member then another. She was a happy content baby and grew into a happy-go-lucky kid who made friends easily. She was usually well-behaved, and we did not have any trouble with her.

Fast Forward...At the age of 16, Faith was sexually assaulted. It was devastating. Not only for her but for her father and I as well. You never realize the far-reaching impact when you hear about crime of any nature. But this one is a crime, and words cannot describe the pain. I remember sitting in the hospital with her for a sexual assault exam, shell-shocked. Thinking that things like this don't happen to us, they happen on TV. It was a crippling feeling for me. I can't even imagine what it was like for her. That crime was a pivotal moment in Faith's life. I used to tell everyone that it was like she took a U-turn after that day. It was like a dark cloud descended upon her. She became withdrawn and would hide in her room. She slept all the time. She lost interest in school where she had been active in cheerleading and doing well. She became defiant and self-destructive. We started her in therapy but as anyone knows, unless someone with mental health struggles wants help...there is little that therapy can do. She was also prescribed medications. But again, without the help of accepting therapy and doing the work, medications are just a band-aid. Besides, I knew in my heart that this was a spiritual battle. About a year later, Faith began to have suicidal ideations. She was even hospitalized for a week. This too was extremely heart-breaking. I will never forget the 2-hour long ride to that hospital following the ambulance taking her. I was listening to Christian radio and praying. It was the first time I heard Danny Gokey's song "Tell Your Heart To Beat Again". The song's first lines are *"Shattered like you've never been before. The life you knew in a thousand pieces on the floor. And words fall short in times like these when this world drives you to your knees. You think you're never going to get back to you that used to be."* And I bawled! This was what was playing out right before my eyes. The song goes on to encourage that God's hand pulls us through. And the story isn't over. This song was PROPHETIC. God had organized this song to play to speak encouragement to me. I knew then that WE were in a spiritual battle. One that Faith was not in a position to fight alone. She was not in a position to fight at all. It was up to me. And my momma-bear came out. I was going to God every day for her to return to God and find peace in him. However, my desires for Faith were dwarfed in comparison to God's desires for Faith. But I did not know that at the time. I just knew that my daughter was in a downward spiral, and it wasn't going to end well if God did not intervene. So, over the next year, I prayed while Faith continued to spiral. The more I prayed the darker the shadows became. It was far worse than I even knew. She went from being suicidal to rebellious. She started staying away from home. She began a homosexual relationship. Since Faith was aware of our biblical stance on homosexuality, she tried to hide it from us by calling this person a "friend." But inside we knew. I tried to talk to her about it, but it was a closed door. I decided that there was little I could do about it and I needed to let God work it out. I did not think that Faith was homosexual. I felt like it was a knee-jerk reaction to the sexual assault and its resulting trauma. I could belabor the issue and lose Faith, or I could let God work it out and win the war. Even typing this testimony, I am struck every time I use her name, how the spiritual implications like "lose faith" are astounding. We had made a mistake upon her return from the hospital, letting her move her room to the third floor. She had been wanting to do that for a while and we thought it would make her happy. As I said, this was a mistake. It gave her "privacy" and removed her from our vigilance. We did not go up there often as we should have and knew precious little about what went on up there. We trusted her when we should not have. God was giving me warning signals, but I only knew to pray harder. She left a bag in the living room one day that I opened and found all these papers. They had been fashioned into a little book. More than a little curious, I started to read and what I saw horrified me. It appeared to be a book of witch-craft spells! There were other alarming items found in her room. I went up one day to clean it because we started having a rodent problem and

I was sure it was due to trash, dirty dishes, and leftover food left in her room. When I got up there, there were all these posters and pictures hanging all over her walls, nearly covering them. The pictures were dark in nature. Words to "songs" that talked about hatred, death, suicide, and pain. It was very disturbing. I ripped them all down which really made her angry. She eventually put them all backup. She was always having her "friend" stay over. I did not know how to stop that without causing a blow-up. We were walking on eggshells because of the suicide threats. Once released from the hospital, she was evaluated for mental health services. She told the lady that she did not see the need for counseling and so the intake worker left saying that she could not be forced into treatment. At the age of 16, in the state of Pennsylvania, by law, anyone can refuse medical treatment including mental health treatment. I was perplexed and dumbfounded. The ONLY tool I had was prayer. But, as you will see, when prayer is all you have, prayer is all you need. Faith eventually agreed to get counseling. She was approved for what they called "wrap-around" services. We had counselors coming to the house 3 times a week. Once for Faith. Once for me, as her support system. And once for the family. It didn't take long for the family counseling to address a family dynamic that had Faith doing as she pleased without consequences from us. We feared her mental health fragility and became lax with rules and consequences. We, again, began to set house rules and firm consequences with follow-through. As I think back on that time, I am reminded of an allegory I heard once at a ministry retreat. *"Say you have a huge pile of putrid trash in your kitchen. You have lived with it so long that you do not even recognize the smell anymore. A friend comes over and says "Man, your house smells. It's because of that trash sitting in the kitchen. We need to clean it up. Come on, I'll help you." You both begin removing the trash, but as you do, the smell gets stirred up and seems to be worse. You now can smell what you couldn't before and say "Stop, you are making it worse." But the only way to get rid of the smell is to completely remove all the trash."* That's what happened. As soon as her father and I started setting firm rules and implementing firm consequences, things went from bad to worse. At one point, I found that she was watching

X-rated movies on Netflix so I changed the password to restrict her access to Netflix. I also changed the password to the wi-fi so she could not access someone else's Netflix account and watch unapproved movies on her phone or computer. She was livid. It was so bad that we had to call the counselors for a special visit. They came and Faith blew up. They backed our decision and her continued disrespect caused another consequence of us taking her phone for a week. Almost as soon as they left, Faith went on a violent rampage throwing things and breaking things and it even escalated to her taking a hammer to use it on me. Her "friend" intervened and she stormed out the door. The police were called because of her mental health issues and her risk for running away or self-harming. Also, the counselors were called and returned to the house. Faith contacted my husband who picked her up and brought her back home for more counseling. Honestly, at that point, I was dealing with my own PTSD triggered by violence aimed at me in an abusive relationship. I wanted her removed. But counseling calmed the storm, although she felt like it was my fault for taking her phone. She owned none of her responsibility in the incident. I knew that I needed help. Like Moses holding his staff up so that the Israelites could defeat the Amalekites, I was getting tired. I needed an "Aaron" and "Hur" to come along side of me and pray for Faith. I needed GOD to move! So I called in reinforcements. There were a couple of intercessors I knew from our previous church that I called and had them come over. I explained the situation and all that had transpired. And we began to storm Heaven. They came once a week for about a month. We went up to her room when she was not there and we prayed. We anointed her walls. We called for warring angels to come and do battle. And a battle it was. Just like the saying that it is darkest before the dawn, as we started to pray things started to appear worse. But I am learning that NOTHING is wasted in GOD'S HANDS! Because of some learning difficulties early on, Faith had been held back in first grade. So at this point, Faith was a senior in high school at this point, even though she turned 18 in October of that year. She began skipping school to stay home with her "friend". She began bucking the rules even more. She would stay out all night and not tell us where she was. At one point she had an intimate relationship with an ex-boyfriend in her bedroom while I was at home. A couple of days later, for some reason, revealed that to me. Trying to remain calm I had a conversation with her to see if she had used contraceptives. She had not. I then tried to ascertain if she could have gotten pregnant. The possibility existed. She told the boy who came to us, much to his credit and said if she was, he would be as responsible as he could be for her. In the end, she had a friend's aunt buy her a Plan B pill. The attitude was that she believed that she could do anything she wanted because she was 18. And our stance was that as long as she lived under our roof, she had to abide by our rules. So at 18, she decided to move out and get an apartment with her "friend". Our hands were tied. She was ill-prepared to be a responsible adult but there was nothing we could do to stop her. So now with no control over Faith, truly my only weapon was prayer. But God is faithful! All my children have been dedicated to God. And if you read the story of Hannah in 1 Samuel 1:9-27. You will see that when Hannah prayed for a son, she promised that the son would be "dedicated" to God. When God fulfilled her prayer and gave her Samuel, he was taken to the temple and dedicated to God. There he lived in service to God. When you dedicate your child to God. It is more than promising to raise them to know God. It is giving them back to God to do with as He pleases. And God keeps his covenants! He will use every situation to bring them back to Him. You can rest on that. I still have Knowing that Faith is in God's hands, I had to leave her in His hands to do as He willed. I continued to pray for her return to God. I knew that the time had come that I had done all that I could do and God had to do the rest. And HE did. I saw that she had some hard knocks coming. Some reality checks were in store. But I also knew that God is faithful and His promises are true.

I cannot even begin to express my gratitude for what God has done in Faith. I believe it's been maybe 2 ½ years ago (my timing could be wrong) that she called me and was telling me how she was led to destroy her tarot cards. She didn't know why but God was telling her to destroy them. I was blown away. You have read her testimony as only she can tell it. God has done an amazing work in her. I have watched her grow spiritually now as I watched her grow physically as a baby. She has grown in so many ways in just a few short years that it took me a lifetime to grow. I am so proud of her and Thankful for all that God has done.

DEDICATION/Shoutouts
Dedicated to God
Shoutouts

1. Debra Burrington (warrior princess prayer warrior that never lost faith in her daughter from the beginning to the end.)
2. Terri Fantasia (prayer warrior)
3. Jane Geeza (prayer warrior)
4. Natasha homeless lady (planted seeds)
5. Johnesha Slata (life savior)
6. Christopher Cooper (evangelist)
7. Yvette Jones (Mentor, Sister, and friend)
8. Jovaun Aponte (walked with me through the good bad and the ugly amazing husband and friend)
9. Melissa Dougherty (safe place, door opener, keys to

I

Chapter 1 Spiritual Deceit

Chapter 1

Understanding the devil is a lie

Chapter 1 (Spiritual Deceit)

In my journey in witchcraft I had to Go through a "spiritual awakening" Spiritual deceit is what I like to call it. Here's how it started for me. I was first informed that we are souls having a human body experience. The concept of this Spiritual Awakening revolves around the notion that you are powerful within yourself and all you need to do is meditate and align your chakras, which would help tap into your so called awakening. After diving deeper into this world of deception I then started learning about using crystals for healing and alignment. If your mind, body, and soul are off balance you would use a corresponding crystal that is charged by the moon, sun, or rainwater. When you see numbers in sequences like 111, 222, or 333- known as "angel numbers" - you will know that you are aligned. Following the angel numbers can lead to tarot reading, runes, and seeking mediums. Now you are hooked to zodiacs, astrology, birth charts, and more. These orders will not always be in the same pattern, but in my situation, this was the case for me.

Understanding the devil is a lie old trick and no magic

Adam and Eve, while in the garden the snake manipulated them by saying, "You will not certainly die." This was demonic deception at its finest. No, they wouldn't die physically but they did die spiritually. The snake tricked Adam and Eve knowing that they would assume that death was physical, not spiritual. Next, the snake told them they would have all-knowing knowledge like God.

4"You will not certainly die," the serpent said to the woman. 5 "For God knows that when you eat from it your eyes will be opened, and you will be like God, knowing good and evil." Genesis 3:4-5

⁶ My people are destroyed for lack of knowledge: because thou hast rejected knowledge, I will also reject thee, that thou shalt be no priest to me: seeing thou hast forgotten the law of thy God, I will also forget thy children. Hosea 4:6

In this case the devil is using the same tactics when it comes to the first steps of your "spiritual awakening." Tricking people into believing that they are powerful in their own strengths. Yes, we are in the human body with the spirit of life breathed into our nostrils but we aren't powerful in our own strengths, *John 15:5 says; "I am the vine; you are the branches. If a man remains in me and I in him, he will bear much fruit; apart from me you can do nothing"(NIV).* After Adam and Eve ate the forbidden fruit they didn't gain knowledge like God.

What is meditation and chakras?

Meditations and chakras originate from Hinduism and Buddhist practices. Mediation is a form of concentration in Hinduism and Buddhism religion. In their practice of meditation, they believe that there are seven vortexes of consciousness; these vortexes are called chakras. They believe that each chakra has its focal point based on its location in the body. For example, the root chakra is located on the base of the spine and represents stability in one person's life. The side effects if blocked a person would be fearful, anxious, and have anxieties about life. When balanced the person would feel safe, secure, and centered. If the chakra is overactive the person would act in greed, lust for power, and aggression.

The second step in "Spiritual awakening", is meditation and aligning chakras with sound

Frequencies because you are imbalanced or your Chakras are closed off. Balancing and opening these frequency points is a temporary destructive way of checking your behavior. Why do I say that because what happens if there is no change what happens if that form of meditation doesn't work? What happens if you are at work in an office or location where you can't sit down and stretch or do yoga? Don't get me wrong Meditation itself isn't bad when done correctly the Bible even mentions it in Joshua 1:8

"Study this Book of Instruction continually. Meditate on it day and night so you will be sure to obey everything written in it. Only then will you prosper and succeed in all you do." Joshua 1:8

I'm sure you're asking why I should listen to an old book. A great acronym I was told was that the Bible stands for basic instructions before leaving Earth. It's better than an old spell book or a passed-down book of shadows. Why do I say that you ask? And I'm sure you can try to argue "Well Buddhism and Hinduism and new age practices were way before the bible." Let me ask you this: would you rather have a flip phone with small buttons or would you rather have the latest phone? I don't know about you but I would rather have the new latest phone. The foundation is the same, it's still a phone but when you compare them both it's easier to see and send text messages on then the other. Just like the new latest phone Jesus gave us an easier way to meditate which is in his word you can keep a scripture on your desk at work or school as a lock screen on your phone and that will give you peace.

I will listen to what God the LORD says; he promises peace to his people, his faithful servants— but let them not turn to folly. Psalms 85:8

Step 3 angel numbers.

Let me ask you where you would go to look to learn more about angels? Wherever in the Bible did it say or demonstrate angels will talk and communicate through a sequence of numbers? Angels delivered messages and warnings and uplifted people and still do till this day but not in a Sequence of numbers. The angel number sequence is 111,222,333,444,555,666,777,888 and 999. If you look up the chart of meaning for each number none of them say the same meaning when looking at this information online. Not to mention the number 666 is the devil's number.

14 "And no wonder, since Satan himself masquerades as an angel of light." 2 Corinthians 11:14

18" This calls for wisdom. Let the person who has insight calculate the number of the beast, for it is the number of a man. That number is 666." Revelations 13:18

While following the angel numbers (demon numbers) they sweet talk you into seeking tarot readings and mediums eventually. Some people skip to the medium part especially if they lost a loved one and want to know if they are okay. Just like Satan, he is the father of lies I sought out a medium to contact my dead brother to see if he was okay and because I Was talking to a Witch I was even more exposed to new-age practices and items in her metaphysical shop.

You belong to your father, the devil, and you want to carry out your father's desires. He was a murderer from the beginning, not holding to the truth, for there is no truth in him. John 8:44

Witches and new-agers are blinded by the enemy; they may even have a family history and claim that paganism has been in their bloodline for years which could very well be the case, but that breaks into the book of Enoch (book before the Bible). When the Watchers also known as fallen angels showed us humans about witchcraft God flooded the earth trying to wipe away mankind because these watchers had offspring with us humans making giants(Nephilim) leaving Noah and his family left, because God found favor In Noah's eyes the practices were still taught but God kept a promise and a covenant with us not to flood the whole earth because he saw mankind to be good.

7 And the Lord said, I will destroy man whom I have created from the face of the earth; both man, and beast, and the creeping thing, and the fowls of the air; for it repenteth me that I have made them. But Noah found grace in the eyes of the Lord. Genesis 6:7:8

Divination

Root word of Divi : separated into parts, divided.

Most tarot readers group their readings by zodiac sign unless it's a one-on-one reading. I remember I wouldn't start my day until I read my horoscope and or watched my favorite daily tarot reader on YouTube just to see how my day was going to be. The readers were telling me how I should act but yet still playing off as encouraging at the same time. The devil was keeping me busy so I didn't have time for the lord instead of reading my word I was spending my time reading horoscopes, instead of watching sermons I was watching videos on how to manifest the devil had me separated from my Godly purpose as well as distracted.

Divination is the practice of seeking knowledge of the future or the unknown by supernatural means. There are various tools to form these practices.

Runes is another form of divination; it was one of the first. The

Jewish Priests carried these runes but they weren't called runes it was called Urim and Thummim the priest used these stones to ask God for guidance when they weren't near the Tabernacle or the altar for God.

It wasn't until Jesus came and died for our sins he was the Ultimate sacrifice. Jesus came and made it very easy for us to communicate with him. We don't need any divination tools to talk to him, just faith and prayer.

6 "I don't want your sacrifices—I want your love; I don't want your offerings—I want you to know me. Hosea 6

Father God in the name of Jesus please forgive me of my sins. Today I'm standing in the Gap for ___ lord please take the scales off __ eyes help ____ to not fall into any spiritual deception that was planted from the enemy. remove and replace any demonic foundation planted in ___ mind and life help ____ to meditate on the things of you Lord , and to follow your will your word and not false teaching in Jesus mighty name I pray Amen.

2

Chapter 2 Faith and Restrictive Thinking

Chapter 2 Faith and Restrictive Thinking

When it comes to worshiping other gods and deities there's a tendency to follow one that best suits our wants. Showing honor by sacrificing or putting out an offering to get a gift or a wish granted by a god. This brings me to my first question.

Question 1: why worship a God and or the universe that can't grant you everything?

False gods are just resources. Why not go to the ultimate source, the God that created the universe?

In the beginning, God created the heavens and the earth. Genesis 1:1

But seek first his kingdom and his righteousness, and all these things will be given to you as well. Matthew 6:33

Offering: a thing offered, especially as a gift or contribution.

Question 2: When setting an offering to a god was the spell granted completely or was it just granted then taken away making it look like an effect that you got what you wished for?

Even through our sins, God will still show grace and Favor to us there was a time in my life before moving out of Pottstown when I was performing a ritual of balance in life God knew the type of person I was and the sins I committed but still showed me favor and grace on helping me to move out of Pottstown to start my new journey with him.

8 And God is able to bless you abundantly, so that in all things at all times, having all that you need, you will abound in every good work. 2 corinthians 9:8

Question 3: did the spell do more harm then good?

The world teaches you to follow your heart's desires but the bible explains that the heart is very wicked and deceitful. Spells are performed with the selfish intent on the person's wants not needs.

For the Lord is good; his steadfast love endures forever, and his faithfulness to all generations. Psalm 100:5

Question 4: Did it leave you empty wanting more?

Now don't get me wrong, witchcraft is real but when you sacrifice rocks, herbs, rain, whatever element, or close treasure to you, you are sacrificing your holy fruits, peace, love, and joy. When I was in witchcraft I was depressed conflicted self harm had thoughts of suicide and murder. Everything was stolen from me. I had no peace. I would sometimes wake up with scratches and would get pulled out of my bed when I was sleeping. Even saw a hat man standing over my bed. I was still confused about why this was happening and continued. The devil doesn't care about what you want, he just wants you far away from Jesus and the truth as much as possible.

36 For what shall it profit a man, if he shall gain the whole world, and lose his soul? 37 Or what shall a man give in exchange for his soul? Mark 8:34-38

Question 5: why worship any God that isn't in our image of us?

"So God created man in his own image, in the image of God created he him; male and female created he them." Genesis 1:27

Worshiping the Faye (fairies), isn't our image As well as mermaids, Hindu gods, Egyptian gods(God before them), and way more.

Your father is the devil, and you do exactly what he wants. He has always been a murderer and a liar. There is nothing truthful about him. He speaks on his own, and everything he says is a lie. Not only is he a liar himself, but he is also the father of all lies. John 8:44

The Bible warns us about Satan's lies. He is the prince of this world that's why we see Disney, Netflix, the Music Industry, and most entertainment involve magic and subliminal messages in the airways music artist on the crosses, zodiacs, goats, keep your eyes open and you shall see.

2 in which you once walked, following the course of this world, following the prince of the power of the air, the spirit that is now at work in the sons of disobedience. Ephesians 2:2

3

Chapter 3 Knowing your identity / not zodiac

Chapter 3 knowing your identity

Chapter 3 *Knowing identity / not zodiac*

Greek mythology was one I was mostly into. Everyone has their preference. I used to be a part of a witches community online and everyone practiced and followed their own. When I was into witchcraft I believed that for each zodiac sign, there was a corresponding god to worship based on your astrological chart. This causes confusion and loss of My true identity.

What is your true identity in Christ?

- **You are blessed (Ephesians, 1:3)**
- **You are chosen (John 15:16)**
- **You are loved by God (Romans 8:38-39)**
- **You are fearfully and wonderfully made (Psalms 139:14)**
- **You are treasured (Exodus 19:5)**
- **You are completely in Christ (Colossians 2:10)**

The tongue has the power of life and death, and those who love it will eat its fruit. Proverbs 18:21

How to break these word curses is to speak life

You can speak life by speaking God's word over you.

So is my word that goes out from my mouth. It will not return to me empty but will accomplish what I desire and achieve the purpose for which I sent it. Isaiah 55:11

Looking back at zodiac signs I don't remember many positive things about each sign. The key points I remember are that Geminis are two-faced and cancers are just babies, Libra is Flirtatious and Taurus doesn't like to share. One thing I look at in the list of naming these qualities is that they are all flaws. When saying "Hey I'm a Pisces " there's a list of word curses you agree to.

Why would you put yourself in a box when you are so much more than that?

Thank you for making me so wonderfully complex! Your workmanship is marvelous—how well I know it. Psalm 139:14

When studying an astrological chart and knowing the moon, the sun rising, and so forth for your zodiac it gets you hooked. I remember when I was so into astrology I wouldn't start my day until I looked at my horoscope app or watched my cards being read for my zodiac sign for the day. If it told me not to get a contract or go for a job or start a business for this day or month I wouldn't because there's a planet that's in retrograde or whatever the case may be saying the universe isn't in my favor. What if I told you that you didn't have to wait? What if I told you that when you first seek the kingdom of God all the things will be added to you?

But seek first his kingdom and his righteousness, and all these things will be given to you as well. Matthew 6:33

I can do all things through Christ which strengthens me. Philippians 4:11–13

Prayer for coming out of False identity and or standing in the Gap let's break False Identity! (replace the blanks with a loved one and or yourself)

Father God, in the name of Jesus, forgive me of my sins knowing and unknowing I'm standing in the gap for ___ I pray that seeds will be planted and ____ will soon understand that they are more than a conqueror through you Jesus. I denounce any agreement that____ came into with zodiac signs and or word curses spoken over____ life I pray that___ walks in their true identity in Jesus Christ I pray Amen

4

Chapter 4 Understanding God's voice vs the Devil's voice

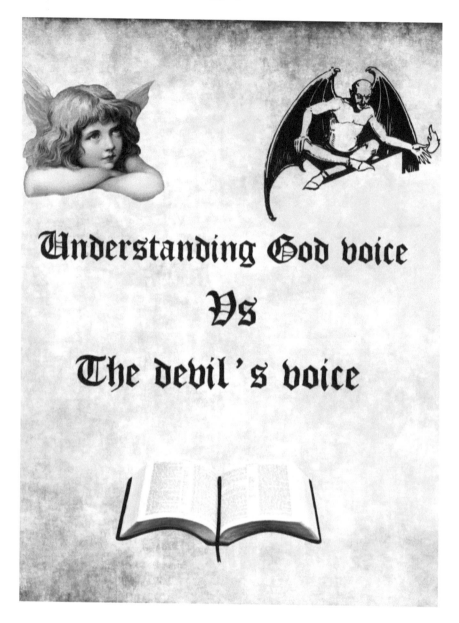

Understanding God voice Vs The devil's voice

Understanding God's voice vs the Devil's voice

Chapter 4

The devil comes only to steal and kill and destroy; Jesus came so that they would have life, and have it abundantly. John 10:10

A lot of people think that God is a horrible God who doesn't care for us at all. I asked and questioned God all the time in the past and asked. "God, why would you let this happen ?" " I thought you were supposed to protect me?" " Do you like to see me suffer? Is this the reason why I'm here ?" Not having a fast response or immediate change made me think that he was evil and didn't care about me at all because he let sexual assault in my life take place. The truth of the matter is that I was lacking in a relationship just because I went to church didn't mean I had a relationship, now I'm not saying here that God let me go through that in my testimony, because I didn't have a relationship with him I'm saying that I wasn't close to my father teaching.

my people are destroyed from lack of knowledge. Hosea 4:6

Here is an important key to having in your life to understand the voices of God Vs the devil. Now people can be used by the devil and People can be used by God. Here is a list that helped me differentiate the two and helped me increase my discernment in people, places, and or things.

Satan's voice

- Rushes you
- Pushes you
- Frightens you
- Confuses you
- Discourage you
- Worries you
- Condemns you

Gods voice

- Calms
- Comforts
- Convicts
- Encourages
- Enlightens
- Leads

- Reassures
- Still

Knowing the nature of how the lord and Satan speak is important. The lord talks in a small still voice while Satan is loud. Have you ever seen a cartoon or a movie with a small angel on one side of the shoulder and a devil on the other side of someone's shoulder? It's like that all the time when it comes to your thoughts and making decisions. Choosing which one you want to listen to is the free will that God has given us.

You, my brothers and sisters, were called to be free. But do not use your freedom to indulge the flesh; rather, serve one another humbly in love. Galatians 5:13

I personally rather serve a God that isn't forced on me and waits patiently for me to come with open arms. Now you can argue and say "But Christians knock on my door and always try to shove their beliefs down my throat." My response to that logic is that Christians aren't God, people that follow Christ found a good thing and they would want to share it with everyone. The pain that we go through in life isn't in vain but to help others enjoy the freedom of salvation.

You intended to harm me, but God intended it for good to accomplish what is now being done, the saving of many lives. genesis 50:20

Church hurt

Church Hurt is a term referencing the emotional scarring, or abuse experienced in a church setting with or among believers Church Hurt can be inflicted, intentionally or unintentionally on another person.

Church hurt is unfortunately very common these days but that doesn't make it right. I had my fair share of church hurt in my journey of Following Christ. One pastor called me a Gigolo but in a female body in front of the whole congregation and I had another pastor from a different ministry who was married tell me that he found me attractive and wanted me to be the prophet of his church. The First pastor Discouraged me and the Second Frightened me whether their intent was intentional or unintentional they were still being used by the devil. The Bible says that we should not forsake the assembling of one another.

Going through that was the testing of my Faith. I had to ask myself, was I Going to church just to fit in? Or was I attending Church to learn more about Jesus? Another way to think about it is this: if you are getting bullied in high school or work ask yourself why are you there to make friends, Or get an education/ paycheck. As a Group of believers, we are called to encourage one another not bring them down.

not giving up meeting together, as some are in the habit of doing, but encouraging one another—and all the more as you see the Day approaching. Hebrew 10:25

Now If Church hurt has taken place in your life and resulted in sexual harassment, and abuse then I recommend leaving and reporting the issue to the police. There are many churches in the world, online churches, and in-person But not all people act like that.

(Let's pray to replace the blanks with your name or a loved one and or friend)

Heavenly Father forgive me of my sins Today I stand in the Gap for ___ I pray the voices of satan becomes slient in ___ life I pray that your voice becomes adamant in __ life . I Pray lord that you heal any form of of church hurt in __ life and you restore any brokenness in ___ heart and mind and or Body and give ____ a heart to forgive In Jesus mighty name I Pray Amen.

5

Chapter 5 Gods and Other Gods

Gods and Other Gods
Chapter 5

In my journey in Newage, I followed many false gods and idols chasing what I wanted or what I thought I needed at the time. Such as Prosperity, love, self-love, peace, luck and more. It didn't matter to me as long as I could get what I wanted. I believed that I was assigned to a god based on my zodiac sign. Even though I still picked whatever one was able to help me with getting what I desired at the time.

Greek mythology Gods were what I looked at the most because of that thinking. What I failed to realize at the time was the fact that the definition of myth.

Myth: Myth is a widely held but false belief or idea.

Myth being the prefix for mythology, did not pay no mind that what I was worshiping was false. False gods like you to think that you are in control of everything and that you have the power to fix any issue. Understanding that healing comes from Jesus and not from oneself or own strength is an important step to complete freedom.

Exposing principality rulers in high places
These false gods are principalities
False Gods claim to be

1. **False God of war**

- Skanda (Hindi)
- Guan Yu (Chinese deity)
- Montu (Egyptian)
- Ares (Greek)
- Mar (Roman)
- Hachiman (Japanese)

Big question to think about : why would there be division if we wasn't in a fallen world?

The devil comes only to steal and kill and destroy. I came that they may have life and have it abundantly. John 10:10

The real war is between the unseen realm against rulers in the unseen realm There is one unseen realm built by fear and the other built by faith both battling one another that is where the war lies. The only one who can give you the keys to help you fight through any battle is Jesus Christ.

while we look not at the things which are seen, but at the things which are not seen: for the things which are seen are temporal; but the things which are not seen are eternal. 2 Corinthians 4:18

The Lord *is* a man of war; The Lord *is* His name. Exodus 15:3

2. False god of love (todays Cupid)

- Kamadeva (Hindi)
- Yue Lao (Chinese)
- Hathor (Egyptian)
- Eros (Greek)
- Venus (Roman)
- Benzaiten(Japanese)

"Beloved, let us love one another: for love is of God; and everyone that loveth is born of God, and knoweth God. He that loveth not knoweth not God; for God is love." 1 John 4:7-8

1. **False gods of protection**

- Krishna (Hindi)
- Nezha (Chinese)
- Horus (Egyptian)
- Soteria (Greek)
- Salus (Romans)
- Hachiman (Japanese)

The LORD himself watches over you! The LORD stands beside you as your protective shade. The sun will not harm you by day, nor the moon at night. The LORD keeps you from all harm and watches over your life. The LORD keeps watch over you as you come and go, both now and forever. Psalms 121:5-8

my God is my rock, in whom I take refuge, my shield and the horn of my salvation. He is my stronghold, my refuge and my savior— from violent people you save me.

4 "I called to the LORD, who is worthy of praise, and have been saved from my enemies. 2 Samuel 22:3-4

You don't have to dig your way around trying to find multiple gods to fill your needs when you can follow Jehovah jireh, the one true God.

Big questions

1. Who is the real God ?
2. Why would you worship or follow a God that can't do it all?
3. Why would you follow a God that isn't made in the image of us?

So God created mankind in his own image, in the image of God he created them;

male and female he created them. Genesis 1:27

Satans Imagery and patterns

Idol: an image or representation of a god used as an object of worship.

Some scholars think that Baal and the Baphomet are the same idol which makes sense Satan can and do take many forms and has been doing that since the beginning of time as we know from Adam and Eve in the garden Satan took a form as a snake disguised as an animal that looked like it belonged in the garden. Do not be deceived. The imagery of Baphomet is as above so below used many times in witchcraft symbolism. Having the Baphomet being a pagan and or gnostic idol, it's used in divination, rituals, and more.

In this image ^ there is a description of a Greek god, Chinese god, Hindi, tarot cards and a so-called image of Jesus all doing the same notion as above so below this symbolism.

"You must not make for yourself an idol of any kind or an image of anything in the heavens or on the earth or in the sea. Exodus 20:4

I am the LORD; that is my name! I will not give my glory to anyone else, nor share my praise with carved idols. Isaiah 42:8

The devil card is displayed as an image of men and women in bondage and chains "as above and below". In new-age teaching "As above so below "comes from the corresponding principle they follow. They believe that what happens above like the stars/zodiac will happen in their mind and on earth physically.

In the beginning, Adam and Eve had everything they needed and more until they were kicked out of heaven after being tricked by Satan.

Satan's motive is to have humans suffer here on earth as well as in hell considering he was casted out of heaven. Satan knows scripture and knows the principle that anyone who practices sin is a slave to sin. To glorify and practice it is and will be damaging to the mind body and soul.

Jesus answered them, "Truly, truly, I say to you, everyone who practices sin is a slave to sin. John 8:34

"How you are fallen from heaven, O Day Star, son of Dawn! How you are cut down to the ground, you who laid the nations low! You said in your heart, 'I will ascend to heaven; above the stars of God I will set my throne on high; I will sit on the mount of assembly in the far reaches of the north; I will ascend above the heights of the clouds; I will make myself like the Most High.' But you are brought down to Sheol, to the far reaches of the pit." Isaiah 14:12-15

Hinduism is the oldest practiced religion in the world but everything dates back to the beginning. Remembering that this world is ruled by Satan. Having false religion established already.

"Again, the devil took Jesus to a very high mountain and showed him all the kingdoms of the world and their splendor. 9 "All this I will give you," he said, "if you will bow down and worship me." Matthew 4:8

This is why you see music artists today talking about sex, drugs, murder, and money. Claiming to sell their soul for fame to get to the top.

Yes, Satan is the prince of this world but God is bigger it is written and it shall come to pass that Satan will only rule temporarily and will be cast back to hell. At the moment Satan is waiting and trying to take as many souls captive, as the devil card shows.

8 Be alert and of sober mind. Your enemy the devil prowls around like a roaring lion looking for someone to devour. 1 Peter 5:8

What do people mean when the end is near?
Top current end times events in the Bible

• Euphrates river drying up

Taken August 30, 2021

"And the sixth angel poured out his vial upon the great river Euphrates; and the water thereof was dried up, that the way of the kings of the east might be prepared. "Revelation 16:12

Rebuilding the 3rd temple

By **BEN SALES**
16 Jul 2013, 12:39 pm |

A young boy standing next to a model of the Second Temple at the Temple Institute in Jerusalem. (photo credit: Nati Shohat/Flash90)

Is it

"He will oppose and will exalt himself over everything that is called God or is worshiped, so that he sets himself up in God's temple, proclaiming himself to be God."2 Thessalonians 2:4

"He answered them, "When it is evening, you say, 'It will be fair weather, for the sky is red.' And in the morning, 'It will be stormy today, for the sky is red and threatening.' You know how to interpret the appearance of the sky, but you cannot interpret the signs of the times. Matthew 16:2-3

Beginning of True transformation tiredness

True Tiredness

Come to me, all you who are weary and burdened, and I will give you rest. Take my yoke upon you and learn from me, for I am gentle and humble in heart, and you will find rest for your souls.

Matthew 11:28

When I was coming to Christ I got to the point where I was just tired. Tired of being depressed and tired of my living situation. Tired of trying to do everything myself. Now my transition is still an ongoing process. I try to die to my flesh daily and the learning never stops. Realizing that I needed to put my faith in God and just be honest and vulnerable to him was one of the keys to freedom and breakthrough. The transformation started with me and my discipline and heart.

Now the works of the flesh are evident: sexual immorality, impurity, sensuality, idolatry, sorcery, enmity, strife, jealousy, fits of anger, rivalries, dissensions, divisions, envy, drunkenness, orgies, and things like these. I warn you, as I warned you before, that those who do such things will not inherit the kingdom of God. Galatians 5:19-21

Now I know it's a lot to give up all that and this verse can seem completely unfun and even intimidating but I will tell you that I am not perfect at all. I sin and slip up from time to time. I thank God for Jesus and his grace.

for all have sinned and fallen short of the glory of God, and all are justified freely by his grace through the redemption that came by Christ Jesus. Romans 3:23-24

Repentance is the action of repenting; sincere regret or remorse.

Have you ever gone to a club or a college party and started to drink alcohol so much that you began to vomit and you said this sentence or something of this nature?

"I'm never drinking again" I sure have and I went back that next Friday and went out and did it again, but At that very moment, you are showing sincere regret and remorse by saying "I'm never drinking again"

With new age, I was very sick and tired of feeling used, abused, and unwanted and my works by my hands weren't helping me with the complete actual freedom that Jesus had for me.

As a dog returns to its vomit, so fools repeat their folly. Proverbs 26:11

(Let's Come out of idol worship and pray this prayer to replace the blanks with your name or a loved one and or friend.)

Father God in the name of Jesus forgive me of my sins knowing and unknowingly I denounce and destroy any agreement made in __ life by worshipping or following any false gods/ idols. Thank you lord for being the one true God because there is no God like you. Open___ eyes to see. let ___ get tired/ weary and to desire your truth and perfect ways make yourself known to ___ in there life in Jesus mighty name I pray amen

6

Chapter 6 Steps on True Healing

Steps on true healing

Steps on True Healing Chapter 6

It was common in the biblical days that people in the new age would sacrifice their children. Not saying every person in the new age does sacrifice children just depends on your practices. In the new age, I sacrificed rainwater and stones. Y'all might not be ready to hear this but from being demonically oppressed and slitting my wrist I sacrificed blood and tears without even knowing it, Because I was under demonic oppression but the doctor called it depression. I was on 3 different medications was hospitalized a couple of times and was admitted once. When I found Jesus and knew for sure I was okay and free I was taken off of my medication. For me, It took me about two years before I got delivered and at times the devil still tries to get me to think I'm still sick or go back to a psych ward.

So if the Son sets you free, you will be free indeed. John 8:36
But He was wounded for our transgressions,
He was bruised for our iniquities;
The chastisement for our peace was upon Him,
And by His stripes, we are healed. Isaiah 53:5

I learned that I didn't have to take on any more pain through self-harm because there is a savior that carries and knows the pain we went through and carried it for you and I.

The thief comes only to steal and kill and destroy. John 10:10

The devil wanted me to take my own life to not share the great news of the gospel. He wanted me to think that I have no purpose or value so that way I wouldn't push through all the things that happened to me in spite of what I did or what happened.

True sacrifice to give

1. *Forgiveness*
   If you want a real challenge, forgiving is an effective sacrifice letting down your pride and ego.
   "For if you forgive other people when they sin against you, your

heavenly Father will also forgive you." Matthew 6:14
Trying to forgive the person who sexually assaulted me was hard but the hardest thing I had to do was forgive myself. Not that I did anything wrong but it was hard and I constantly kept beating myself up for it for letting it happen. Forgiveness is a key factor to practice all the time because, at the end of the day, everyone makes mistakes whether big or small it doesn't matter who you are Christian, witch or warlock, lukewarm, saved, and or preaching we all make mistakes. When I was at this stage in my life I was so worked up I would curse and fuss and say "I'm not going to ever forgive what that person did or how they treated me." Something that helped me with the process is what God showed me.

So when I was in a new age and came to my "spiritual awakening " they would say "You are a soul having a human body experience." Which was the truth but we can be used as vessels filled with demons as well. So I had to understand that it wasn't the Person, it was the spirit within them that was trying to come for me, the same one that kills, steals, and destroys.

"For our struggle is not against flesh and blood, but against the rulers, against the authorities, against the powers of this dark world and against the spiritual forces of evil in the heavenly realms." Ephesians 6:12 Something the spirit of God told me right before I was going to work I might add was that All Molestations are rooted in witchcraft I asked God to explain and the spirit told me it was manipulation and control I broke down and cried and he told me it wasn't my fault. Manipulation and control are rooted in witchcraft a lot of sexual assaults happen whether it happened by a family member or whoever for example in one case someone being young or just not knowing 9 times out of 10 the rapist said " Don't Tell anyone because.... lies, lies, and

more lies. As much as I would like to say what that person did to me in the spring of 2016 was worse than what I was doing but, honestly was just as bad it was both operating in manipulation and control A.K.A witchcraft. It was hard to grasp how Jesus forgives us no matter how big or small the sin is but in his eyes sin is sin. not measured in a way we humans measure if Jesus can forgive us why can't we forgive one another and ourselves? *Jesus said, "Father, forgive them, for they do not know what they are doing. Luke 23:34.*

2. *Clean out*

To show that there was a true sacrifice I had to do a cleanout, not a cleansing when you take sage or incense, and "clean" all the negative activity. Because smudging just brings more demons to your area. A cleanout is when you get rid of all of your witchcraft and new-age items out of your house and off your possessions. I cried like a baby. I went on Facebook Live and cut every tarot card up and didn't have a lighter so I tried to submerge them in water.

No one came up and told me "Hey I want you to get rid of these witch tools because it's a sin." The lord had just been talking to me about it in his small still voice. I would lie if I said I didn't go back and buy more after that. I loved reading them but now I fear the lord and don't do that anymore.

The second time I didn't cry but I did have this beautiful crystal ball and I didn't want to get rid of it. I wasn't good at using it. I was trying to master how to use it at the time but God had a different plan. All my crystals, incense, sage, witch herbs, candles, chakra bracelets, books and much more. Getting rid of all these items was showing God that I didn't want to have it my way. I want to have it his way and I trusted him.

"Do not turn to mediums or necromancers; do not seek them out, and so make yourselves unclean by them: I am the Lord your God. Leviticus 19:31

For rebellion is as the sin of divination, and presumption is as iniquity and idolatry. Because you have rejected the word of the Lord, he has also rejected you from being king." 1 Samuel 15:23

It's not just cleaning out materialistic things either; it's cleaning out what's in your heart and realizing you are a sinner. A lot of people come to the New Age because not only is it a selfish practice but because it does not illuminate the person's sin. New age gives false light in a person's life but you will continue to live in darkness unless you confess you are a sinner and in need of a savior. So cleaning out sin looks like confession and laying down to the Father and not picking it back up and walking in faith that you are saved.

3. *Healing process/ deliverance*

deliverance: the action of being rescued or set free.

Now this healing process isn't with Reki healers or crystals or spells. This healing process is through Jesus Christ. Jesus was nailed on the cross and his spirit was given to us to help us with our relationship with God and to help others and welcome them into the kingdom of God.

And if the Spirit of him who raised Jesus from the dead is living in you, he who raised Christ from the dead will also give life to your mortal bodies because of his Spirit who lives in you. Romans 8:11

The Lord is close to the brokenhearted

and saves those who are crushed in spirit. Psalms 34:18

He heals the brokenhearted and binds up their wounds. Psalm 147:3

The Lord sustains him on his sickbed; in his illness, you restore him to full health. Psalm 41:3

There are a lot of Bible verses on healing. In witchcraft, it's the right idea but the wrong format instead of speaking spells over you. You would want to speak Bible verses over you because you have life and death in The power of the tongue and his word does not return to him void.

So shall My word be that goes forth from My mouth; It shall not return to Me void, But it shall accomplish what I please, And it shall prosper in the thing for which I sent it. Isaiah 53:5

The tongue has the power of life and death, and those who love it will eat its fruit. Proverbs 18:21

Having faith is important as well but you only need to have faith as small as a mustard seed that you may be healed abundantly. In this case it will be a position of trading Faith, what you used to put your faith in doesn't serve you anymore so now we put our faith in God. I once used to put my faith in reading my daily horoscope everyday but now I have faith that God will make a way for me even through my words this time.

For truly I tell you, if you have faith the size of a mustard seed, you will say to this mountain, 'Move from here to there,' and it will move; and nothing will be impossible for you." Matthew 17:20-21

Giving burdens to Lord

Have you ever been told to take a deep breath in And a deep breath out ? Giving your burdens to the lord and saying "God I give this anger to you I don't want it " or God I give this feeling of worry to you or loneliness to you I don't want it is a great way of letting go of your burdens.

Now I'm not going to sugarcoat anything if someone does me wrong. I tend to reminisce about it over and over again. When I was in high school I was in an altercation and I disliked this girl . Long after the altercation was over I would go home and a week would pass and I would still be thinking of that one encounter I had with this person. I would even think and say "Oh I should have done this or that." Having that spirit of anger build up in me, harvesting in my soul.

Yeah now that I'm walking with Jesus I still have to give my anger to the lord maybe 11 times a day and keep it pushing until it's no longer on my mind to show God this battle isn't mine and I don't want to carry this anger or move out of the line of what he has called me to do. Now fist fighting was the old me. I fight in the spirit the best thing to do is to let God handle my battles not karma Do who karma is but God got. You may not always see what God does for you when he has your back but just know he is working it out for your good and putting justice on every situation in his perfect timing.

22 Give your burdens to the LORD, and he will take care of you. He will not permit the godly to slip and fall. 23 But you, O God, will send the wicked down to the pit of destruction.

19 Do not take revenge, my dear friends, but leave room for God's wrath, for it is written: "It is mine to avenge; I will repay, says the Lord. Romans 12:19

7

Chapter 7 Your true calling and position!

True calling and positions

There are many examples of Jesus delivering people in the Bible and we are called to do the same.

17 And these signs will follow those who

believe: In My name, they will cast out demons; they will speak with new tongues; 18 they

will take up serpents; and if they drink anything deadly, it will by no means hurt them; they will lay hands on the sick, and they will recover."

People who work in the new age and claim to be reiki healers are really called to lay hands on the sick and cast out demons. Heal people from past trauma, sickness, infidelity and so much more. Everyone is called to do this according to the word of God but 9 times out of 10 "reiki healers " are called to a special office and were made to work for the Holy Kingdom. Same with tarot readers, witches, warlocks, mediums, and more we are all prophetic by nature.

4 *The Spirit clearly says that in later times some will abandon the faith and follow deceiving spirits and things taught by demons. 1 Timothy 4:1*

7 *But to each one of us grace has been given as Christ apportioned it.*

8 *This is why it says: "When he ascended on high, he took many captives and gave gifts to his people."*

9 *(What does "he ascended" mean except that he also descended to the lower, earthly regions?*

10 *He who descended is the very one who ascended higher than all the heavens, in order to fill the whole universe.)*

11 *So Christ himself gave the apostles, the prophets, the evangelists, the pastors and teachers,*

12 *to equip his people for works of service, so that the body of Christ may be built up*

Ephesians 4:7-12

To tap into your true calling you would need to be filled with the Holy Spirit.

And Peter said to them, "Repent and be baptized every one of you in the name of Jesus Christ for the forgiveness of your sins, and you will receive the gift of the Holy Spirit." Acts 2:38

Do not be deceived of Christian witchery you should not mix them Jesus came as an ultimate sacrifice so we do not need to use divination tools.

I am the LORD; that is my name! I will not give my glory to anyone else, nor share my praise with carved idols. Isaiah 42:8

For at one time you were darkness, but now you are light in the Lord. Walk as children of light Ephesians 5:8

Question: what do light and dark have to do with each other?

Again Jesus spoke to them, saying, "I am the light of the world. Whoever follows me will not walk in darkness, but will have the light of life."

John 8:12

Father God in the name of Jesus forgive me of my sins known and unknown Lord I pray that ___ will be able to tap into the plans you have for them (Jeremiah 11:29) I break and come out of Agreement with any false future ___ maybe have or is walking into. I pray that ___ will be filled with the true anointing that you have for ___ life in Jesus mighty name I pray Amen

8

True calling and positions

There are many examples of Jesus delivering people in the Bible and we are called to do the same.

17 And these signs will follow those who

believe: In My name, they will cast out demons; they will speak with new tongues; 18 they

will take up serpents; and if they drink anything deadly, it will by no means hurt them; they will lay hands on the sick, and they will recover."

People who work in the new age and claim to be reiki healers are really called to lay hands on the sick and cast out demons. Heal people from past trauma, sickness, infidelity and so much more. Everyone is called to do this according to the word of God but 9 times out of 10 "reiki healers " are called to a special office and were made to work for the Holy Kingdom. Same with tarot readers, witches, warlocks, mediums, and more we are all prophetic by nature.

4 The Spirit clearly says that in later times some will abandon the faith and follow deceiving spirits and things taught by demons. 1 Timothy 4:1

7 But to each one of us grace has been given as Christ apportioned it.

8 This is why it says: "When he ascended on high, he took many captives and gave gifts to his people."

9 (What does "he ascended" mean except that he also descended to the lower, earthly regions?

10 He who descended is the very one who ascended higher than all the heavens, in order to fill the whole universe.)

11 So Christ himself gave the apostles, the prophets, the evangelists, the pastors and teachers,

12 to equip his people for works of service, so that the body of Christ may be built up

Ephesians 4:7-12

To tap into your true calling you would need to be filled with the Holy Spirit.

And Peter said to them, "Repent and be baptized every one of you in the name of Jesus Christ for the forgiveness of your sins, and you will receive the gift of the Holy Spirit." Acts 2:38

Do not be deceived by Christian witchery you should not mix them Jesus came as an ultimate sacrifice so we do not need to use divination tools.

I am the LORD; that is my name! I will not give my glory to anyone else, nor share my praise with carved idols. Isaiah 42:8

For at one time, you were darkness, but now you are light in the Lord. Walk as children of light Ephesians 5:8

Question: what do light and dark have to do with each other?

Again Jesus spoke to them, saying, "I am the light of the world. Whoever follows me will not walk in darkness, but will have the light of life."

John 8:12

Father God in the name of Jesus forgive me of my sins known and unknown Lord I pray that _ _ _ will be able to tap into the plans you have for them (Jeremiah 11:29) I break and come out of Agreement with any false future _ _ _ maybe have or is walking into. I pray that _ _ _ will be filled with the true anointing that you have for _ _ _ life in Jesus mighty name I pray Amen

9

Full Armor V.S Protection Charms

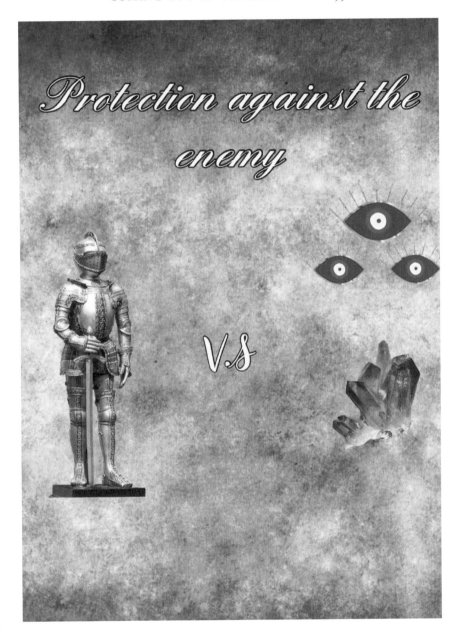

The full armor of God is a form of spiritual protection that people in Christ use to protect themselves from the enemy. Knowing that the enemy comes to harm us with our mental state, physical state, and everything in between. The lord left us all instructions on how to stay protected when going into battle or just our everyday way of life. Written in Ephesians 6:10. The shoes of peace, the sword of the spirit, the belt of truth, the shield of faith, the breastplate of righteousness, and the helmet of salvation and the garment of praise. Each of these pieces of armor holds a purpose. Going into battle without one is dangerous because it leaves you open for the enemy to attack that spot. For example, if I forget the belt of truth the devil can attack me and tell me I'm not good enough or strong enough to get through life but the truth is that " *I can do all things through Christ who strengthens me.*" *Philippians 4:13* But if I forget the truth then I'm open for torment. Not to mention if I forget my belt that's keeping my armor together all of the armor is liable to break or fall off during battle. It's important to understand that we live in a fallen world and that this isn't our end destination.

How to equip the full armor

Pray this prayer

Father God Equip me with the Holy armor of God the chest plate of righteousness, belt of truth, helmet of salvation, sheild of Faith, shoes of peace; sword of the spirit and the garment of praise. That may any issue that comes against me will not harm me in any way Amen

In new age practices, there are protection spells, crystals , amulets, charms, and a lot of other things that try to claim that it will protect you but the truth is it's not practical. Compared to the full armor the full armor is free and reusable compared to the evil eye where you buy the charm or it may be passed down to you and it later breaks and you have to go buy a new one. Creating a spirit of fear and anxiety if you accidentally forget your protection charm at home or rock or whatever can invite worry or fear in someone's life. This isn't to get confused with a cross that people wear around their neck. A cross is a reminder that Jesus died on the cross for our sins so we may have eternal life.

Evil eye is a charm used in today's modern-day used as a protection charm. The Egyptians had a pharaoh named Menes also known as

Horus using an ancient Egyptian eye to represent protection and healing. In 1208 B.C. that is when the Israelites were guided out of slavery by Moses God had stuck Egypt with 10 plagues. Until the pharaoh had no choice but to let his people go. Which led them to make a covenant with the one true God. The evil eye or the ruler at the time couldn't even stand a chance with the living God and a lot of people are using the evil eye as a fashion

statement and for protection. If the " Pharaoh", the so-called "god of protection" couldn't protect himself What makes you think his charm can?

As mentioned in Chapter 5, God is the God of protection

Have you ever heard of the saying "Fight fire with fire ?" ")With hex spells or revenge spells that's exactly what you are doing, filling your heart with anger and bitterness.

38 "You have heard that it was said, 'Eye for eye, and a tooth for a tooth.] 39 But I tell you, do not resist an evil person. If anyone slaps you on the right cheek, turn to the other cheek also. 40 And if anyone wants to sue you and take your shirt, hand over your coat as well. 41 If anyone forces you to go one mile, go with them two miles. 42 Give to the one who asks you, and do not turn away from the one who wants to borrow from you. Matthew 5:38-42

It takes real power to show love in a situation when someone wrongs you. The world will teach and say "Well hurt people hurt people." God tells us if someone is hurting, surrender and show love.

The law of attraction isn't a pagan thing it's actually in the Bible first and it's called the law of the prophets it also was stated multiple times in the Bible in many ways.

"So whatever you wish that others would do to you, do also to them, for this is the Law and the Prophets. " Matthew 7:12

"You shall not take vengeance or bear a grudge against the sons of your own people, but you shall love your neighbor as yourself: I am the Lord." Leviticus 19:18

"And as you wish that others would do to you, do so to them." Luke 6:31

"Hatred stirs up strife, but love covers all offenses. "Proverbs 10:12

The reason why the " law of the prophets" works is because it is written in the Bible and Satan just calls it the law of attraction. The law of attraction wasn't a thing until 1855 in a book called The Great Harmonia, written by the American spiritualist Andrew Jackson Davis. Now I'm not saying that this writer is Satan or the devil, I'm saying this person is confused and confusing others by taking pieces of the Bible and not sharing the rest

Whether knowing or not knowing.

You may not see any harm in just sharing the law of the prophets but not calling what it is opens a door to people leaving a lot of misinformation out leaving people stuck and confused.

I thought it was okay to be a "good witch" as long as I wasn't hurting anymore. Not realizing that I was hurting myself I had no real protection, no armor or guidance to get through my Everyday life. Even with that, there is division. I know people in a new age who would defend their case that they are good witches and don't bring harm to others but love and light and I was one of them who would claim this as well. The division between Good witches and bad witches can and will cause a spiritual altercation. In the body of Christ, there is no division; we are all one body on the same mission.

that there may be no division in the body, but that the members may have the same care for one another. 1 Corinthians 12:25

Father God in the name of Jesus forgive me of my sins knowingly and unknowingly I pray that __ put(s) complete trust in you. I pray that ___ will be able to walk in love letting there be no division in the body of Christ. Let ___ walk into freedom from all anxieties in ___ life I pray for the full armor of God in ____ life give ____ the knowledge to fight. In Jesus mighty name I pray Amen

10

Claircognizance vs Gifts of the holy spirit

Claircognizance vs Gifts of the Holy Spirit

Claircognizance vs **Gifts of the holy spirit**

In mediumship practices, it is taught that there are 5 abilities that you can tap into number one is clairvoyant having or claiming to have the power of seeing objects or actions beyond the range of the natural vision. Number two clairaudience is the power of hearing something not present to the ear regarded as having objective reality. Number three is the paranormal ability to taste a substance without putting anything in one's mouth. Those who process this ability can perceive the essence of a substance from the spiritual or eternal realm through taste. Number four is the ability to access psychic knowledge by smell. Lastly, number five is Clairsentience when you can pick up on other's emotional energy and feel a shift in the emotional space. Each of all five of these new age practices is activated by meditation emptying yourself and opening the corresponding chakra points to open these abilities. Emptying yourself can be dangerous because you are allowing other spirits in through the five senses for you which could lead to schizophrenia, torment, depression, anxiety and so much more.

2 You know that when you were pagans, somehow or other you were influenced and led astray to mute idols. 3 Therefore I want you to know that no one who is speaking by the Spirit of God says, "Jesus be cursed," and no one can say, "Jesus is Lord," except by the Holy Spirit. 1 Corinthians 12:2-3

When filled with the holy spirit you operate in gifts that are clean and holy given by God.

Finally, brothers and sisters, whatever is true, whatever is noble, whatever is right, whatever is pure, whatever is lovely, whatever is admirable— if anything is excellent or praiseworthy—think about such things. Philippians 4:8

There's a right way to do things and a wrong way to do things God will be able to justify it in his word. Jesus healed the sick of many people with mental illness, the lame, blind, and so much more. Jesus made a way for us to have his spirit here on earth by dying on the cross for our sins.

17 In the last days, God says, I will pour out my Spirit on all people. Your sons and daughters will prophesy, your young men will see visions, your old men will dream dreams. Acts 2:17

You can also receive the Holy Spirit by repentance and baptism.

Peter replied, "Repent and be baptized, every one of you, in the name of Jesus Christ for the forgiveness of your sins. And you will receive the gift of the Holy Spirit. Acts 2:38

4 There are different kinds of gifts, but the same Spirit distributes them. 5 There are different kinds of service, but the same Lord. 6 There are different kinds of working, but in all of them and in everyone it is the same God at work. Now to each one, the manifestations of the spirit is given for the common good. 1 Corinthians 12:1

These gifts are given out to build up the church God's people as well as people God is trying to call whether they are in a church building or out church building. The gifts of the holy spirit are wisdom, understanding, counsel, fortitude, knowledge, piety, and fear of the Lord.

2 The Spirit of the Lord will rest on him

the Spirit of Wisdom and of understanding,
the Spirit of counsel and of might,
the Spirit of the knowledge and fear of the Lord
3 and he will delight in the fear of the Lord.
Isaiah 11:2-3

Compared to Claircognizance and its 5 functions the holy spirit moves kind of like the 5 functions the only difference is that the New Age is moving and manipulating and mocking the holy spirit through the spirit of the Antichrist.

*What spirit do you want to move under?

4 but every spirit that does not acknowledge Jesus is not from God. This is the spirit of the antichrist, which you have heard is coming and even now is already in the world. 1 John 4:3

When I was in the world and tried to open up these clairvoyant abilities I didn't realize I was filled with an antichrist spirit. Nothing can compare to the holy spirit. Now with the holy spirit, I feel whole and brand new and have help with my everyday life and loving guidance.

Unlike Claircognizance, the gifts of the holy spirit are given by God not of works of man meaning it's not called to meditate or have certain crystals(rocks) to allow you to open up to tap into certain gifts. The gifts are given to you at an appointed time by the Father to encourage, warn, and help others through trials and tribulations in one person's life.

11

Chapter How to Be Filled With The Holy Spirit

Why do we need the holy spirit?

Jesus' ministry did not start until he was baptized and filled with the holy spirit.

13 Then Jesus came from Galilee to Jordan to be baptized by John. 14 But John tried to deter him, saying, "I need to be baptized by you, and do you come to me?"

15 Jesus replied, "Let it be so now; it is proper for us to do this to fulfill all righteousness." Then John consented.

16 As soon as Jesus was baptized, he went up out of the water. At that moment heaven was opened, and he saw the Spirit of God descending like a dove and alighting on him. 17 And a voice from heaven said, "This is my Son, whom I love; with him I am well pleased."

Matthew 3:14-17

Later performing miracles of healing people from sickness and diseases of who was willing to follow.

3 Jesus reached out his hand and touched the man. "I am willing," he said. "Be clean!" Immediately he was cleansed of his leprosy.

Matthew 8:3

Without the holy spirit we will not be able to walk out our true purpose in life.

15 He said to them, "Go into all the world and preach the gospel to all creation. 16 Whoever believes and is baptized will be saved, but whoever does not believe will be condemned. 17 And these signs will accompany those who believe: In my name, they will drive out demons; they will speak in new tongues; 18 they will pick up snakes with their hands; and when they drink deadly poison, it will not hurt them at all; they will place their hands on sick people, and they will get well."

Mark 16:15-18

21 "Not everyone who says to me, 'Lord, Lord,' will enter the kingdom of heaven, but the one who does the will of my Father who is in heaven. 22 On that day many will say to me, 'Lord, Lord, did we not prophesy in your name, and cast out demons in your name, and do many mighty works in your name?' 23 And then will I declare to them, 'I never knew you; depart from me, you workers of lawlessness.'

Matthew 7:21-23

(Let us stand in the Gap and or pray to be filled, replace the blanks with a loved one name and or your own.)

Father God in the name of Jesus forgive me of my sins knownly and unknowingly I pray that you encounter ___ and fill ___ with your holyspirit I pray that you touch on ___ heart to be baptized and or refilled with your Holyspirit and never leave ___ or forsake ___ in ____ journey in walking with you In Jesus mighty name I pray Amen

12

Chapter 12 Divination tools VS Prophetic Gifts

During my first deliverance before coming to Christ, there was this man and he was known to be an Apostle of this revival I attended. This Apostle I never met before and didn't know but this man of God was able to tell all of the things about my past without even using any divination tools. My faith lifted after that and demons started to manifest to the point I had no control over my Body the demons were then cast out and the next thing I knew I was free. That apostle was flowing and operating in his calling and prophetic gift. After the deliverance, I still could never understand why or how he was able to tell me everything about myself without using any divination tools or even knowing me but now I know that he was called and flowing through the holy spirit.

3 On the other hand, the one who prophesies speaks to people for their upbuilding and encouragement and consolation.

1 Corinthians 14:3

Divination Tools

Pendulum: A stone(crystal) on a chain used for reiki healing, communication with the dead, and or finding missing items.

When I was in New Age, I would take my pendulum with me everywhere I would ask questions on tests and even ask for it to point and swing to where my missing keys were. Holding it over my hand asking the stone to show me what yes looked like then it would swing in one direction then asking the stone to show me what no looks like then it would swing another way.

Carrying that pendulum I realized I was communicating with familiar spirits. Same with having a pet as a familiar to help with witchcraft potions and rituals. Whether unseen or seen, it's still an unfamiliar spirit at work.

6 And the soul that turneth after such as have familiar spirits, and after wizards, to go a whoring after them, I will even set my face against that soul, and will cut him off from among his people. Leviticus 20:6

Familiar spirits are demons that are assigned to you that know your every move their assignment is to get you off course kill your joy and have you far away from Jesus's love and freedom. Using any form of divination tool it's keeping you away from your true calling because divination tools are a direct access point to the demonic spirits.

13 Saul died because he was unfaithful to the LORD; he did not keep the word of the LORD and even consulted a medium for guidance,

14 and did not inquire of the LORD. So the LORD put him to death and turned the kingdom over to David son of Jesse. 1 Chronicles 10:13-14

Being part of them practices had me suicidal and had me inflict self-harm I would constantly feel like no matter what I did I just wasn't happy.

4 Saul said to his armor-bearer, "Draw your sword and run me through, or these uncircumcised fellows will come and abuse me." But his armor-bearer was terrified and would not do it; so Saul took his own sword and fell on it.

5 When the armor-bearer saw that Saul was dead, he too fell on his sword and died.1 Chronicles 10:4-5

It's crazy to even think that I used to be so into scary movies like The Conjuring watch how people get possessed and then later look up the history of the event the movie took place and videos of Ed and Lorraine Warren museum of haunted items they have like dolls voodoo dollars, cursed items all from witchcraft or rooted in a cult practices but yet I still messed with divination tools. Instead of familiar spirits, it's better to be guided with the holy spirit. You don't need any tools to be guided in your everyday life when walking with Jesus, just the word of God in your heart so the spirit can bring it to your remembrance.

But the Helper, the Holy Spirit, whom the Father will send in my name, he will teach you all things and bring to your remembrance all that I have said to you. John 14:26

Scrying (crystal ball)

Crystal ball: a solid globe of glass or rock crystal, used by fortune-tellers and clairvoyants for crystal-gazing.

When I was studying how to use a crystal ball I had a new age book that told me to practice by looking in the sky and seeing if I could try to make out any shapes in the clouds above. A crystal ball, tea leaves, divination cup, bones, and water are all used for scrying. It's like staring blankly at something and trying to make shapes and letting your imagination take over. *Casting down imaginations, and every high thing that exalteth itself against the knowledge of God, and bringing into captivity every thought to the obedience of Christ; 2 Corinthians 10:5*

Whether you are in the kingdom of darkness or not it is still written. Satan likes to take and contort Your true calling in Christ and pervert it for his kingdom confusing others and taking them farther away from people's true calling. Satan needs a vessel so the images and predictions seen are not images given by the holy spirit but by the Antichrist spirit.

In the old covenant in the bible yes they used divination tools but in the new covenant, Jesus came and sent his spirit so we will not need to use any of the divination tools. Back then God guided the Israelites in the sky

21 By day the Lord went ahead of them in a pillar of cloud to guide them on their way and by night in a pillar of fire to give them light so that they could travel by day or night. Exodus 13-21-22

That is why in witchcraft there is a flame nearby when using a crystal ball. To reflect a light but that light isn't needed and isn't as bright as Jesus' light this is one example of the devil's mocker.

John 8:12. When Jesus spoke again to the people, he said, "I am the light of the world. Whoever follows me will never walk in darkness, but will have the light of life."

Using a crystal ball light is needed to get a reflection and a prediction but God knows the plans he has for us.

11 For I know the plans I have for you," declares the Lord, "plans to prosper you and not to harm you, plans to give you hope and a future. Jeremiah 29:11

Just by opening up the word of God you will begin to get a better understanding and revelation of what is to come to pass in every season of your life.

5 If any of you lacks wisdom, you should ask God, who gives generously to all without finding fault, and it will be given to you. James 1:5

Tarot cards

With first starting out in tarot cards every deck comes with a little booklet to read with instructions and what each card means whether drawn out right side up or upside down. Nothing can compare to the things of God. There are 78 cards in a tarot deck but compared to the word of God there are 66 books in the holy bible so much more revelation in your life and so much guidance in your life so that way you can and will be able to live more abundantly.

Father God in the name of Jesus forgive me of my sins knowingly and unknowingly I pray for _ _ _ that there is an understanding thats divnation tools and clairvoyance is a mockery of the holyspirit help_ _ to not trust in physical things and newage items and fous on things of you. I denounce and bind any agreement that _ _ _ made by seeking out palm readers , tarot readers , fortune tellers , any witch or warolck. I pray that _ _ _ bloodline will be covered by the blood of christ breaking any curse that may of fallen on _ _ _ in Jesus mighty name I pray amen.

13

Chapter 13 Denying self

Denying self

Denying self/flesh

This walk in Christ is not easy. I'm not going to lie and say it's a piece of cake, this walk is not for the weak but I'm sure by faith you will be able to conquer this part. Practicing witchcraft is all about self desires. Now don't get frustrated and give up and close this book. This is hard for me even today. Realizing I can't get my way all the time but I can overcome this struggle with Jesus Christ. When I was a little girl my mom would say "The world doesn't revolve around you!" She would say that to me so many times I couldn't count. Being adopted at a very young age, spoiled, and the youngest hey I think you would get very full of yourself quickly also I would ask for something and get what I wanted there were times when I was younger I would ask my mom for something and she would say no then I would ask my dad for something and he would say yes. Little did I know I was operating under witchcraft manipulation it worked but I caused a lot of altercations between my mom and dad lot at the time I didn't seem to care because I got what I wanted not realizing that I was being selfish and not looking at the big picture and sadly it took me 20 years to figure that out.

I always had a big heart for people. I always gave up my stuff. I had to help someone else who was less fortunate than me. When I came to Christ and got fully delivered I

realized that i had something that no one else really had and I want to share it with everyone and that is freedom.

"So if the Son sets you free, you will be free indeed." John 8:36

I didn't even know that there was this type of freedom and this freedom I wouldn't trade it for the world literally. One thing I will do is share the great news of Jesus Christ a lot of people can say "Yeah I went to church I haven't really felt anything" and or even attended small groups I did this and that with church but it didn't work for me But did you know that this is freedom is hidden to the people that their hearts are hardened and don't truly believe.

And even if our gospel is veiled, it is veiled to those who are perishing. 4 The god of this age has blinded the minds of unbelievers, so that they cannot see the light of the gospel that displays the glory of Christ, who is the image of God. 5 For what we preach is not ourselves, but Jesus Christ as Lord, and ourselves as your servants for Jesus' sake. 6 For God, who said, "Let light shine out of darkness," made his light shine in our hearts to give us the light of the knowledge of God's glory displayed in the face of Christ. 2 Corinthians 4:3-6

When I went through the traumatizing event of sexual assault it was just the last straw and icing on the cake for me I didn't believe that Jesus wasn't able to save me I didn't understand his true power and love. With that event happening to me I didn't understand why God let this happen to me. He loved me so much but God gave us free will. So unfortunately if I wanted to go punch someone in the face I could punch someone in the face. So why would God do a crazy thing like that? The answer is that he loves us. Allow me to explain if we were forced to worship and bow down to God like clockwork our love wouldn't be true. In the book of Exodus, there was a king named

Pharaoh and he would work the Israelites like a Dog day and night but it wasn't until Moses came along and made away for them to be free from captivity. Moses had a great relationship with God and they gave honor to God and worshiped him freely and their love was true. We all go through tough things in life but Jesus can save and heal he just waiting for you to seek and find him.

Ask and it will be given to you; seek and you will find; knock and the door will be opened to you. Matthew 7:7

Unfortunately, the devil did a great job of knocking me down I wanted to end my life and tried a couple of times it been like that for 6/7 years battling with depression, and suicidal thoughts but God wouldn't let me he knew that I would be strong enough to keep going. Whatever you are going through I know that you are strong enough to keep on going. I promise you that it isn't easy on your own but you will be free and delivered from it if you stay close and true to the savior in Jesus' name.

no weapon forged against you will prevail, and you will refute every tongue that accuses you. This is the heritage of the servants of the LORD, and this is their vindication from me," declares the LORD. Isaiah 54:17

So when it comes to denying yourself the basics it's understandable it's not about you. My heart is burning even saying that to myself it makes me so mad inside but you just gotta keep going. There are some things I'm still working on also but I know that God has begun a good work in me and I know no matter what he will finish it and he will finish it in you also.

And I am certain that God, who began the good work within you, will continue his work until it is finally finished on the day when Christ Jesus returns.Philippians 1:6

For my thoughts are not your thoughts,
neither are your ways my ways,"
declares the Lord.
9 "As the heavens are higher than the earth,
so are my ways higher than your ways
and my thoughts than your thoughts.
10 As the rain and the snow
come down from heaven,
and do not return to it
without watering the earth
and making it bud and flourish,
so that it yields seed for the sower and bread for the eater,
11 so is my word that goes out from my mouth:
It will not return to me empty,
but will accomplish what I desire
and achieve the purpose for which I sent it.
Isaiah 55:8-11

The heavens are higher than the earth. Why worship the earth rather than the heavenly father? when the sexual assault took place in my life I turned to believe in healing in rocks(crystals) but they didn't promise me anything Isaiah 55 verses 12- 13 talks about the promise we will have when we put our complete trust in God and not trying to out-think him or know his ways.

12 You will go out in joy
and be led forth in peace;
the mountains and hills
will burst into song before you,

and all the trees of the field

will clap their hands.

13 Instead of the thornbush will grow the juniper,

and instead of briers the myrtle will grow.

This will be for the Lord's renown,

for an everlasting sign,

that will endure forever."

Isaiah 55:12-13

I needed to have faith and lean on the word of God that jesus is going to handle it.

he Lord works out everything to its proper end—

even the wicked for a day of disaster.

5 The Lord detests all the proud of heart.

Be sure of this: They will not go

Proverbs 16:17

Father God in the name of Jesus forgive me of my sins knowingly and unknowingly I pray that _ _ _ _ will walk into letting down any pride and letting you lord take the wheel in _ _ life lord I pray that this battle and walk to freedom will succeed in everyway even if _ _ doesnt see that everything is working for _ _ _ good lord I pray that you continue to walk with them to the end in Jesus mighty name I pray Amen.

14

Beware of Witchcraft in churches

Witchcraft in churches

Getting connected.

Getting connected to a church is important to someone who could help you along the way so that way you can be taught how to fight against the enemy. Be washed clean of your sins with baptism. Fellowship and so much more. Compared to being part of a Wiccan covenant or pagan schools and learning about colors and their meanings and zodiac signs and useless information with the right church it will help you live a life abundantly with full potential. I recommend a church especially if you were into a new age to connect with a deliverance ministry or a 5-fold after channeling spirituals and other demonic rituals it would be key to complete freedom and having someone experience and perform a deliverance session.

25 not giving up meeting together, as some are in the habit of doing, but encouraging one another—and all the more as you see the Day approaching. Hebrews 10:25

I don't think an exorcism

Is the way to go but deliverance is. when Jesus

came and delivered the many people, he didn't throw a cross at anyone and tell the demons to leave, He simply said women you are free. Then the woman was free.

When Jesus saw her, he called her over and said, "Dear woman, you are healed of your sickness!" Luke 13:12

You say you have faith, for you believe that there is one God. Good for you! Even the demons believe this, and they tremble in terror. James 2:18

Don't think that you are safe in Churches there are ministries out there and church leaders that can and do operate in Witchcraft. Witchcraft is rooted in control and Manipulation. Here are three things to watch out for.

1) Control in the church

When a Church leader or member of the church tells and forces you to behave in a certain way outside of the church.

My example I Was part of a Ministry where I couldn't work a certain place Because of the fact I wasn't able to come to church on a midweek event every Tuesday although I had off Sunday. I also wasn't allowed to conversate with any of the men in the church outside of the congregation Unless it was supervised by a Leader and if we got caught hanging out it was a public rebuke on Sunday while the church was live.

2) Manipulation in church

When a Pastor, Teacher, Preacher, and or Leader Holds a "prophetic "message from you until you give on to the ministry or sow a Seed.

Witches do that if you want a personal tarot reading you pay Even if you walk on the beach and see them automatic fortune tellers you need to put money in first. **"God so loved the world that he** *gave* **his only begotten son that whoever believes in him shall not perish but have everlasting life- John 3:16 "** *God gives not expecting anything in return if the spirit of God leads you to give on to a ministry and you personal feel lead then you go ahead. Yes, the bible talks about sowing onto a ministry and a place that feeds you but my question is Did God tell you first about sowing? A Prophetic word should never be new news it should be a confirmation that always lines up with the word of God and its true given context.*

Emotional Giving in churches (manipulation)

Emotional giving is when a church leader and or pastor gives a sob story about how they cannot afford the lights and or the building to keep it running and then continue to ask for money week after week for the same issue and may even give the members of the church a set price to give. Don't get me wrong it is important to give tithes and offerings to the church but in this case, when it comes to emotional giving (manipulation) It takes discernment. Paying a tenth of your tithes is important due to the fact it shows your trust in God. When I was in New Age I put my trust in so many tangible things I spent lots of money on tarot cards and crystals becuase that is where I put my trust in at the time. God asked me a question and still asks me to this day sometimes "Why is it you can trust all these things and spend your money on meaningless stuff but can't put away and your trust in me?"

I would spend my time setting out offerings to false gods and not the true living God that personal eye-opening experience for me is what caused me to give, not because some Pastor, teacher, Preacher, etc. told me but becuase God placed it in my heart.

6 Remember this: Whoever sows sparingly will also reap sparingly, and whoever sows generously will also reap generously. 7 Each of you should give what you have decided in your heart to give, not reluctantly or under compulsion, for God loves a cheerful giver. 2 Corinthians 9:6

Paul warns and explains how preachers with unpure motives in Philippians 1:15-18

15 It is true that some preach Christ out of envy and rivalry, but others out of goodwill. 16 The latter do so out of love, knowing that I am put here for the defense of the gospel. 17 The former preach Christ out of selfish ambition, not sincerely, supposing that they can stir up trouble for me while I am in chains. 18 But what does it matter? The important thing is that in every way, whether from false motives or true, Christ is preached. And because of this, I rejoice. Philippians 1:15-18

Although I had my fair share of being in other churches that controlled and boasted in themselves and operated in control and manipulation among members I forgave the leaders and still thank God that the word of God was preached. I learned a valuable lesson in all this I don't go to church for leadership/ people I go to church for Jesus and to learn the word I later had an encounter with the holy spirit and my eyes were open and led me on the right path and I Thank God for sending his spirit and to help and lead me out and guide me along to this day.

15

Chapter 15 Verse for battle

Verses for battle
(you are ready !)

Don't rush the process of the walk with Christ stay on track and increase your discernment and most importantly build that personal relationship with God stay encouraged with all that being said I leave you with my last Question Are you Ready to come out of Witchcraft?

What to read when you feel .....

Angry

- *19 My dear brothers and sisters, take note of this: Everyone should be quick to listen, slow to speak, and slow to become angry, 20 because human anger does not produce the righteousness that God desires. 21 Therefore, get rid of all moral filth and the evil that is so prevalent*

and humbly accept the word planted in you, which can save you.
James 1:19-20

Anxiety/Worry

- *25 "Therefore I tell you, do not worry about your life, what you will eat or drink; or about your body, what you will wear. Is not life more than food, and the body more than clothes? 26 Look at the birds of the air; they do not sow or reap or store away in barns, and yet your heavenly Father feeds them. Are you not much more valuable than they? Matthew 6:25-26*

Depressed

- *"I waited patiently for the Lord; he inclined to me and heard my cry. He drew me up from the pit of destruction, out of the miry bog, and set my feet upon a rock, making my steps secure. Psalms 40:1-2*

Doubt
"The grass withers and the flowers fall, but the word of our God endures forever Isaiah 40:8
Fear
not fear: I am with you; do not be anxious: I am your God. I will strengthen you, I will help you, I will uphold you with my victorious right hand. Isaiah 41:10
Guilty
If we confess our sins, he is faithful and just to forgive us our sins and to cleanse us from all unrighteousness. 1 John 1:9
Lonely

- *Keep your lives free from the love of money and be content with what you have because God has said,"Never will I leave you; never will I forsake you." Hebrews 13:5*

Taken for granted

- *Whoever walks in integrity walks securely, but whoever takes crooked paths will be found out.*

Proverbs 10:19

Suicidal thoughts

- When the righteous cry for help, the Lord hears and delivers them out of all their troubles. The Lord is near to the broken-hearted and saves the crushed in spirit. Many are the afflictions of the righteous, but the Lord delivers him out of them all. He keeps all his bones; not one of them is broken. Psalm 34:17-20
- The Lord will fight for you, and you have only to be silent." Exodus 14:14
- For I know the plans I have for you, declares the Lord, plans for welfare and not for evil, to give you a future and a hope. Jeremiah 29:11
- No temptation has overtaken you that is not common to man. God is faithful, and he will not let you be tempted beyond your ability, but with the temptation, he will also provide the way of escape, so that you may be able to endure it. 1 Corinthians 10:13

Fear

- *For God has not given us the spirit of fear, but of power and of love and of a sound mind. 2 Timothy 1:7*
- *There is no fear in love, but perfect love drives out fear because fear has to do with punishment, and so one who fears is not yet perfect in love. 1 John 4:18*

Unwanted

- God decided in advance to adopt us into his own family by

bringing us to Himself through Jesus Christ. This is what he wanted to do, and it gave him great pleasure. 1 Ephesians 1:5

unattractive/ ugly

- So God created mankind in his own image, in the image of God he created them; male and female he created them. Genesis 1:27

Milton Keynes UK
Ingram Content Group UK Ltd.
UKHW021224160324
439484UK00004B/65